Don't Pull the Chicken Switch

How to Maximize Willpower and Get Everything You Want Out of Work and Life

By Kit Allowitz

Copyright © Kit Allowitz 2017

All Rights Reserved.

ISBN: 978-0-9991684-1-7

No part of this publication may be reproduced or transmitted in any form or by any means, mechanical or electronic, including photocopying and recording, or by any information storage and retrieval system, without permission in writing from the publisher.

Request permission for or further information on usage of this document should be addressed to:
kit.allowitz@chickenswitching.com

Legal Notice

The Purchaser or Reader of this publication assumes responsibility for the use of these materials and information. Adherence to all applicable laws and regulations, federal, state and local, or any other jurisdiction is the sole responsibility of the purchaser or reader.

The author and publisher assume no responsibility or liability whatsoever on the behalf of any purchaser or reader of these materials.

Any perceived slights of specific people, characters or organizations are unintentional.

Jacket design by Michael Matera – michael.matera@gmail.com

…..for all those I have pulled the chicken switch on and caused pain

….. this book about powerful willpower lessons is written in story form.

Everyone likes a good story. Enjoy.

Kit Allowitz

Contents

Chapter 1	Trouble at Trio
Chapter 2	Pre
Chapter 3	Cups
Chapter 4	Marshmallows
Chapter 5	Present and Future Self
Chapter 6	First Reports
Chapter 7	Slugs, Curls and Long Runs
Chapter 8	Temptation
Chapter 9	Genetics and Resources
Chapter 10	Procrastination
Chapter 11	Speaking Up
Chapter 12	Dolphins, Integrity and Belief
Chapter 13	Contentions
Chapter 14	Fred
Chapter 15	Lifeline
Chapter 16	Stories
Chapter 17	Amends
Chapter 18	Epilogue: Race
Chapter 19	Conclusions and Summary of Lessons

Chapter 1: Trouble at Trio

Mark Buczkowski, Trio Inc's CEO, was watching his executive team argue ... again.

"No way," said Roger, the vice president of sales. "Never."

Roger pointed at Trio's conference room walls, which were cluttered with a variety of freshly hung posters that called for action.

"Come on," Eddie argued back. "You know as well as I do that our people need to get out of neutral. This is the third quarter in a row that our numbers are down. We've tried incentives, spot bonuses, we've tried being *nice*, and nothing has changed. We need to show our people that we're putting our foot down, and this is the best way to do that."

Eddie, the chief operating officer, and Roger continued to argue as the other executives examined the posters Eddie had put up on the wall. The largest had Eddie's head Photoshopped onto the body of Tim "The Tool Man" Taylor from the 90s show *Home Improvement*, with Tim's signature catchphrase "more power" changed to "More Willpower!" Another showed Roger and Mark as the *Saturday Night Live* characters Hanz and Franz with the tagline "Pump Up Your Willpower!"

Linda, vp of finance, gazed at a medium sized poster of herself as Oprah Winfrey. In the poster she was pointing with both hands and shouting "YOU get more willpower ... EVERYONE gets more willpower!" Other posters had the rest of the executive team as celebrities with similar messages.

One of the larger posters was labeled "Rules For Willpower," and was full of statements such as:

- More Hours = More Willpower = More Money = More Success
- If The Sun's Still Up, Keep Working
- Breaks Are For the Weak. Work Harder!
- Willpower Never Runs Out, So Neither Should You
- Toughen Up And Use Your Willpower 24/7

Mark traded a look with Albert, vp of human resources, who was shaking his head in concern. Before Mark could ask Albert's opinion, Roger spoke up: "Mark, you have to agree how counterproductive these posters will be."

"Mark, will you *please* tell Roger to stop being such a stick-in-the-mud," Eddie shot back, mimicking Roger's tone.

"Okay, that's enough," Mark said, standing. Roger dropped into his chair, glaring at Eddie. Eddie sat too, helped along by a direct look from Mark.

"Now," Mark continued. "A month ago, we decided unanimously that we needed to do something to turn our numbers around, especially after last quarter. We decided on the theme of *willpower*, because we believe many of our problems are because our people aren't following through on company goals and expectations when we need them to.

"Eddie volunteered to come up with an idea, and this is it. Clearly not everyone here agrees with the posters, but let's discuss the idea like mature adults okay?"

"Fine," said Eddie airily. "You all know I'm right. Roger's just scared to look silly on a poster."

"That's not it at all," Roger said.

"Whoa," Mark said. "Eddie, you know Roger is careful sometimes. But he's no dummy. If he thinks this might not work, he probably has a good reason. I ask you to hear him out. Roger, if you have issues with Eddie's idea, then I would like to ask you to spell them out clearly. Is that okay?"

There were grudging nods in response.

"Eddie, let us make sure we understand your idea," Mark continued. "The plan is to put up these posters all over the building, and use them to show our employees that their leaders want them to work harder, stay longer hours, be more productive, and generally up their game to get more done so that we can turn our numbers around. Correct?"

Eddie nodded. "The part I like is that when it comes down from all of us together, no one can ignore it."

Lori, Trio's vp of marketing spoke up. "Can I say something? I do think the posters are clever. They will definitely grab our employees' eyes. And making fun of ourselves a bit won't hurt. Eddie's right that many departments could be working harder."

"I like them too," said Linda, admiring the poster of herself. "I always wanted to be Oprah." The serious mood in the room lightened a touch at the joke, and even Eddie and Roger smiled. "Seriously though," she added, "I like the idea of more willpower. I know I could use some more of that at the gym. Maybe we all could use more of it around here too."

Mark made sure no one else was waiting to speak. "Okay, now does anyone *not* like Eddie's posters as they stand?"

Roger raised his hand. "Personally, I think the posters are silly and undermine our authority, but it's not just that. Lori, you may think some people need to work harder, that's fine. But my salespeople are already working their rear-ends off. They're making more prospecting calls now than they did last quarter, the one before that, and the one before that. I'm getting complaints about long hours, and now Eddie wants me to go back and say work even harder? I'd have a mass walkout in ten minutes."

"I'm not a fan either," Trina, who ran facilities, put in. "With our numbers down this far, we've had to cut hours in my department. My warehouses are down to two shifts, which means fewer people and more for them to do. Telling them to just work harder will *not* go over well, especially since longer hours aren't an option with our hourly folks."

"And that's not the worst of it." Albert from HR leaned forward. "Eddie, I agree that improving our willpower could help all of us, but do you have any idea how many calls I'll get when that list of rules goes up? No breaks, longer hours, staying after dark, and with the bosses supporting the idea? That's like the industrial revolution all over again. We won't just get walkouts, we'll get lawsuits. And that's in the three minutes before the press gets hold of it, not to mention our competition! I'm all for more willpower, but this isn't the way to make it happen."

"Maybe we'll lose a few people, but maybe we need to," countered Eddie. "If people can't or won't work as hard as they have to for Trio, maybe they shouldn't be here in the first place. Taking steps like this to motivate our teams is what we wanted wasn't it?"

Eddie looked around the room, trying to find support. Albert, Trina, and Roger were not on board, that was obvious, but even Linda and Lori were looking uncomfortable.

Mark took control of the meeting. "Eddie, we all appreciate the effort and thought you put into these posters," he said, "but in light of the issues the team has just mentioned, I'm afraid we can't put them up in their current form. I have to make the decision, and it's a no-go."

Eddie sighed. "All right, fine. But we've tried a bunch of other things and none of them have worked. We're running out of time.

How long do you think our investors will be patient with us? Another quarter or two like the last three, and we're all done, so if these posters aren't the answer, someone else better tell me what is."

"I don't have a problem with the willpower part." said Trina. "I think improvements on that front, in this room, and company-wide could help a lot." The others nodded, even Roger. "But like Albert said, there's got to be a different way to go about it. I mean, one of your posters says that willpower never runs out. That doesn't seem reasonable. I think we need to make it clear what exactly it is we want from our employees before demanding changes across our entire organization."

Roger grinned and cocked his head slightly. "And Eddie, you know I love you like a brother, even when I want to smack you one, but there's a difference between increasing willpower and just working harder. We can't just assume that the second equates to the first."

"Do we even know what willpower means in the context of our organization?" asked Albert. "I've heard so many different definitions; I'm not even sure what it is we're trying to get people to do. I know we want results, but what kind of willpower will drive that?"

Linda nodded. "I have the same question. What if we tackled the willpower issue more directly? Figure out what it is and how it works here, then bring that back to our departments to implement? I'd be in favor of that."

Eddie rejoined the conversation, still a little sullen. "Okay, so what if we did? You all don't seem to know any more about how to drive willpower in our people or you would have said so. We're still at square one."

"Maybe not," said Mark. "I think I know someone who could help. Eddie, you, Roger and I worked with a guy years ago, when we were teenagers, long before we started Trio. You remember the peppermint farm? His name is—"

"Wait, you mean Pre?" Eddie interjected. "I haven't even seen him for like twenty years. *He's* going to help us?"

"Maybe," said Mark. "He still lives here in Portland. I bumped into him a few months ago on a run. I was feeling pretty overwhelmed at the time. We ended up sitting on a bench and talked for quite a while. I left that conversation with some knowledge and tools that I could use to put more focus, commitment and discipline into my work and family life. I even gained a couple critical insights on self-improvement and motivation."

Mark looked around the room. "For those of you who don't know him, his given name is Steve Adams. He's an old friend who is seriously into running. When you run as far and as often as Pre does, you definitely learn a lot about willpower. I don't know if he's the right guy to help us as a company, but I know he helped me personally that day, and I trust him."

Eddie spoke up, "I hate to be a naysayer—unlike *some* people (he glared at Roger)—but the last thing we need is an outsider who knows nothing about our business coming in and pointing out everything we are doing wrong—or what he *thinks* we are doing wrong. We've got a complex business."

"Eddie doesn't like criticism," said Roger. Eddie rolled his eyes in response.

"Gentlemen," Mark corrected, "let's focus. I'd like to reach out to Pre this week. If he thinks he can help give our people a little more understanding of willpower, or at least educate us on where to start, I'll invite him to the next meeting. Everyone okay with that? Show of hands?" Everyone's hand went up except Eddie's.

"Eddie?" asked Mark.

"All right, all right. Bring him in. But when this idea falls flat just like all the other ones, you better believe I'll be saying I told you so—and we will be getting these posters back out."

When the meeting broke up a few minutes later, Mark went back to his office. As he passed his assistant's desk, he paused, "Jared, what do I have first thing the next few days?"

Jared tabbed over to his boss's online calendar. "You've got calls through the morning tomorrow, and a pitch rehearsal for a new client with Roger first thing day after, but on Thursday you're open until 10:30. Why?"

"Block out Thursday morning until 10. I'll be coming in a little late that day."

"Sure thing, Mark. Everything okay?"

"Everything's fine," Mark said. "I just have someone important to catch on the running trail." With that, he tapped his assistant's desk twice and disappeared into his office.

Chapter 2: Pre

The following Monday, the group of Trio executives assembled once again in the conference room. Mark was the last to arrive, accompanied by a tall man wearing jeans and a blazer and carrying a small duffel bag. The man smiled as he saw Roger and shook his hand warmly. He then approached Eddie and attempted to greet him, but Eddie just gave an offhand nod, his hands were full pouring himself a cup of coffee. The man persisted and finally got a handshake and hug.

"Good morning, everyone," Mark began as the executives turned their attention to him. "I know we've got several items on the agenda today, but since our guest was gracious enough to take time out of his morning to speak with us, I'd like to start with him. For those of you who don't already know him, the gentleman to my left here is Steve Adams, better known to us as Pre."

Pre smiled a wide grin at the executives seated around the table, winking at Eddie.

"As we discussed last week," Mark continued, "Pre is here to help us with the idea of willpower. I'm hopeful that his approach, while a bit unconventional, can help Trio. I know he's helped me. Pre, thanks so much for being here. The floor is yours."

"Thank you, Mark," said Pre. He had a quiet but clear voice. "I'd like to start by explaining who I am and how I know what I do about willpower. Then we'll talk about Trio's dilemma, as I understand it from what Mark has told me. Finally, I'd like to give you a snapshot of what working with me to solve this problem will look like. Everyone good with that agenda?"

There were nods around the table. Even Eddie looked interested in spite of himself.

"Excellent!" said Pre. "First of all, I don't have any kind of degree in willpower—who does? I'll be the first to tell you that there are probably people out there who know more about corporate motivation than me. I'm not a psychologist, a therapist, or a life coach. I spent a lot of time leading businesses that did quite well, thanks to a lot of people's help, and these days I try to pay-it-back by spending my time helping others get their businesses on track.

"As Mark said, I tend to approach these things a bit unconventionally. Mostly what I am is someone who has been fascinated by finding the limits of my own capabilities. And willpower? Well, what those who wish to succeed use to push themselves to find their own limits."

Pre took a deep breath and continued. "Mark might have told you where I got my nickname. Steve Prefontaine, most called him Pre, was one of the greatest American runners in history, and he was also a fanatical student of self-discipline. Steve wasn't always the fastest out of the gate, but where many of his competitors succumbed to the temptation to slow down, yielding to the strain long distance running has on the body, or the fatigue of their minds, Prefontaine refused to let his body perform at any less than maximum. He ran just as hard at the end of the race as he did at the beginning, and that was his secret. I became fascinated by Prefontaine and his willpower.

"I couldn't stop raving about Prefontaine to everyone that would let me, so people began calling me Pre. His example spurred me to read books about how to cultivate my own determination, and I challenged myself to increase my willpower daily. I even tried to push my other teenager friends at the time to explore their own willpower, but for some reason most of them didn't want to go on ten-mile runs with me after long harvest days on the peppermint farm. Pre smiled at Roger and Eddie.

"By the time I finished high school, I thought I had my drive and determination for running figured out, and then I joined the Air Force."

Albert and Lori, who had both served their country, shared a knowing glance.

"Mark told me you two are former military," Pre said, nodding in their direction. "The military challenged my perspective about willpower and helped me learn how to harness it, to focus it.

"In the Air Force, I eventually became an F-16 fighter pilot. It was in the cockpit that I learned the most powerful lesson about willpower that my tour of duty would teach me, the one that's stayed with me ever since."

Several executives leaned forward expectantly.

"Here it is: *Don't pull the chicken switch.*"

Pre paused for a moment, letting the odd phrase sink in.

"Remember the 80's film *Top Gun?*" he asked. Each hand went up, except Linda's. She shrugged. "I don't see many movies," she explained, almost apologetically.

Pre smiled. "Not a worry. The rest of you, what did you learn from that movie?"

"You never leave your wingman," said Roger.

"Talk to me, Goose," said Trina, and everyone chuckled. "That teaches me we should communicate with each other."

"I learned that Kenny Loggins' song, *Danger Zone*, will get stuck in your head for hours," said Eddie.

"All valid points," laughed Pre. "Another thing that many people pick up on from the movie is something I learned as a pilot: there's an ejector switch in every plane that shoots the pilot, with parachute, into the air, saving his or her life but destroying the plane. Anyone want to guess what pilots call that switch?"

"How about 'chicken switch?'" asked Albert. "I was in the Navy, but I remember our pilots talking about the same thing."

"Exactly," said Pre. "Now clearly, if your plane is going down and there's nothing you can do, there's no shame in ejecting. Not at all. But fighter pilots take it as a major point of pride to eject only as an absolute last resort.

"Pulling the chicken switch was something we trained long and hard to avoid. We were trained, exhaustively, to attempt all other options before bailing out."

Pre went on to explain that fighter pilots flew at twice the speed of sound, were trained to evade enemy fire, all while trying to ignore the thought that they might die at any second.

"A fifty-million-dollar plane, our lives, taxpayer money, and our egos were all on the line every time we strapped ourselves in. The exhaustive flight drills, to the point where I could have executed them blindfolded, helped me stay safe. The lesson I learned from this grueling practice continues to help me today to keep my focus, conquer my fears, and see a mission through—whatever it may be."

The room was quiet now. Everyone listened closely.

"Here's where I'm going with this," said Pre. "Pilots train themselves to have the willpower not to pull the chicken switch in one of the most life-threatening situations a human being can find themselves in. If we can do that, then anybody can cultivate the willpower for themselves to see their own projects through. It just takes practice, awareness, and commitment."

Pre looked around the room. "Who has tried to diet recently. Well, maybe don't raise your hands, but you know what it feels like.

Maybe you're trying to eat healthy but feel as if you can't resist the craving for a doughnut ... or two. That sound familiar to anyone?

"Or, maybe you are trying to complete a project. You've had a long day and need to keep pushing through but you just don't have the drive. That sound familiar at all?"

Pre paused. "Willpower likely manifests in different ways for each of you. Most of the time when we bail on an important task, a plan, or a goal in our lives, there's a critical moment when we had decided to quit, to pull the chicken switch. Resisting this temptation means knowing how to set yourself up to win, knowing how willpower works, and knowing how to call on your willpower when you need it the most. It means training yourself to use willpower effectively. This way, when that crucial moment of decision arrives, you follow through, you complete your task or goal, and you have the willpower to avoid pulling the chicken switch."

"Everyone with me so far?"

Heads nodded.

Mark raised his hand. "Pre, let me interject for a moment. This is terrific stuff, but I'm sure there are a few people around the table who are wondering what this has to do with us at Trio."

"Perfect segway," said Pre. "I hear your company numbers have been falling for the last few quarters and you've agreed that improving willpower might help turn things around. I happen to agree with that, in principle. In practice, it's never quite that simple. If you say you have a willpower issue, I say that somewhere along the line you and your people are pulling chicken switches."

"I'd like to help you identify those chicken switches and train yourselves to stop pulling them. And when I say *you*, I mean those of you around this table. Also, there are more than 750 employees at Trio, and while I may speak to them briefly or in a workshop, my real contribution will be with you."

Pre paused and focused on each person in turn.

"I'm sure that each of you has at least one chicken switch that you pull just about every day. Honestly, who doesn't? I'm willing to bet that some of the switches that each of you pull are also getting pulled in each of your departments. Why? Because the way your followers see you will directly influence the way they work for you. When your own chicken switches are identified and you start making it a habit to avoid them, this company's numbers will turn around rapidly. I've seen it in my own business and in the businesses of others I have helped out. That is all I'd like to offer today before we get started."

Pre stepped back from the table and smiled. "Thanks for listening to me this morning. Questions?"

Pre traded a quick grin with Mark, then nodded to one of the Trio executives who raised his hand. "Yes? Albert, right?"

Albert nodded and asked, "So I get it, you've become an expert of sorts in understanding why people don't follow through. So, how are you going to know what chicken switches we are pulling?"

"I'll only know what your switches are if you tell me."

"Yeah, but what if we don't know them ourselves?" asked Lori.

"Trust me, you already know them. You may not know how to articulate what's wrong yet, but you do know what's happening. I'll give you the tools to identify your switches," said Pre.

Trina leaned in, "What if my switch isn't the same as my department's switch? That make sense? What if my people have a different chicken switch? Or what if there are multiple switches in my department? Each of us oversees lots of employees. I can't imagine we're all pulling the exact same chicken switches."

Pre nodded. "Great question, and you're right, not all of them will be the same. But that doesn't mean the way *you* face problems is not affecting your team. Solving a leader's issues will do a lot more for followers than you might think, even if they don't share the exact issue."

"So what will our day-to-day interactions look like with you?" asked Linda. "Most of us have had some sort of coaching before, but you said you're unconventional. How?"

"That's another good question," said Pre with a smile. "I'll start by offering two of my unconventional how's. One, rather than working on one of your ambitions or on the accomplishment of a goal, I will help you learn what you are doing to keep yourself from meeting your goals. The second unconventional how has to do with where we will be meeting and discussing your chicken switch."

"Which means exactly nothing," mumbled Eddie. "Answer me straight Pre: How can you guarantee that any of your chicken switching mumbo-jumbo will work for Trio? I'm betting you can't."

Eddie turned to Mark. "This company can't afford to throw good money away on psychobabble."

The other executives seemed taken aback by Eddie's criticism, but Pre took the chance to interject.

"Eddie, instead of telling you about my own business's track records and my assistance with other organizations, or even how I worked with our friend Mark here, how about I take your bet? I say this process can make a difference, a big difference for Trio. But, if you win and I can't do what I say, not only will Trio owe me nothing, but I'll make a sizeable donation to your favorite charity … in your name. Deal?"

14

Eyebrows were raised around the table, and it seemed Eddie could barely keep his jaw shut.

"Alright, I guess I can respect that," Eddie added. "But what happens if I lose? Not that I'm going to."

"If you lose and Trio's numbers turn around ..." Pre paused for a moment, considering. "... then Eddie, you have to come on a run with me, at the time and place and distance of my choosing, without complaining once."

"Ha! You're on," Eddie said.

Mark chuckled, "If Pre is really onboard with working under those conditions, I recommend that we bring him on board."

"Hell, I'll second that," said Eddie. "When I'm right, we'll revisit my ideas again."

"Anyone object?" asked Mark. Six heads shook.

"Excellent," he continued. "Pre, let's get started."

"Ready when you are," Pre said, smiling.

Chapter 3: Cups

Pre stood and smiled at the executives, retrieving a duffle bag from under his chair. "Give me just a second to set up." He walked to the head of the table, put the bag down on one corner, and took out four red plastic cups. He placed them upside down in a row on the table.

Eddie squinted at the cups for a moment. "Wait, you're going to do magic tricks, aren't you?"

"Just one trick," Pre said, waving his arms to the room and gesturing theatrically at the four cups. "Ladies and gentlemen, this is another one of the ways I see myself as a bit unconventional. I don't claim I can perform magic on your lives, because you'll do that yourselves, but I do want to begin my willpower training with a display of magic, nonetheless. You see before you four empty cups."

Pre lifted each cup to the group, proving they were all empty.

"These four cups are your introduction to willpower" he added. "There are four of them because in my experience, there are four different ways people look at willpower; four theories about how willpower works, and one of them is false."

Eddie opened his mouth to interject, but Mark placed his hand on his arm.

Pre continued: "The first theory of willpower is represented by this first cup, and it says that willpower never runs out. When you think you're tapped out, it's all in your head. You can push through and find more willpower deep inside. Ever heard that theory?" A few heads nodded.

Pre tapped the first cup with two fingers.

"The second cup represents the theory that willpower is genetic. You are born with a certain capacity for willpower, like you are born with a certain amount of athletic talent or musical talent. Think about Usain Bolt. He was born to run sprints fast, right? Well, just like that, a person may have more or less willpower, or even none at all, but how much you have is part of your DNA from day one." Pre tapped the second cup. Lori and Roger exchanged a look across the table.

"The third cup says that willpower is a day-to-day resource. You have a limited amount of it to start with, but you can develop more over time. On a daily basis, however, you have to ration out your willpower carefully. Once it's gone, it's gone until you can replenish it with something like a good night's sleep or a healthy meal." Pre tapped the third cup. Trina raised her eyebrows and nodded.

"The fourth cup says that willpower is a function of appropriate balances of physiological and psychological factors. These factors increase or decrease your willpower based on things such as personal integrity, repetition of good habits, proper nutrition, a healthy belief system, and self-care and self-knowledge. When you train your body and your mind, know yourself, are true to yourself, and believe in yourself, willpower follows. When you don't, willpower is a struggle." Pre tapped the final cup. Albert and Linda seemed to agree with this idea, as they were nodding.

"Over the next few months," Pre continued, "I will talk about each of these willpower paradigms in more depth, and we'll figure out how to work with some of them to maximize your willpower and minimize the pulling of chicken switches. But first things first: one of these four theories is not accurate and not workable. Three of them are generally accurate, depending on several factors we'll get into soon. Any guesses as to which one of the four is false, not workable, not correct?"

"The last one!" declared Eddie immediately. "Why would staying true to yourself mean that you're going to succeed? I could be a lazy slob and stay true to myself, but that doesn't mean I'm going to have willpower."

"You bring up an interesting example there Eddie. I'm glad you mention it, let's talk about it. True or false, the Ford F 150 you have in the parking lot is a sophisticated array of pieces and parts that if the major components of the truck don't work together and all do their jobs, the truck will not function?"

"Yes, if you are talking major truck components, that's correct," replied Eddie.

"You may still get performance out of the truck for a time if smaller parts and pieces are broken, like a small oil leak or failing clutch, but left unattended, overtime, even these small issues will cause truck failure. In the same fashion, if your physiological and psychological systems, the major operating systems of the body are out of harmony and balance with each other, the system will not perform at optimal levels. This out of balance is called incongruence. A system out of congruence can't work at optimal output. You might find your body can perform with varying degrees of willpower if you are a lazy slob, but just like the oil leak or failing clutch, it will sub optimize willpower over the long run. Over time, systems out of congruence will break down and no longer work optimally."

Eddie approved of Pre's answer with a nod and the discussion continued.

"I think it's the second cup," said Linda. "I know genetics play a role, but I believe in nurture, not nature. You can be born with disadvantages and overcome them."

"Maybe the first one?" put in Albert. "I've had plenty of days where I wish I could keep going but I'm just out of gas."

"All good guesses," said Pre. "Willpower is a tough subject to nail down, and I've heard people previously guess all four theories as false, not workable, or not correct."

"So let's see which one really doesn't work, starting with the first guess." He tapped the fourth cup again. "Eddie, you think it's cup number four, that willpower doesn't run on practice, repetition, and integrity." Pre lifted the cup, revealing a tiny potted plant with a purple bloom, which Mark, Roger, and Eddie immediately recognized as a peppermint plant. There were a few gasps around the table, and a "Whoa!" from Lori.

"Sorry, old buddy," said Pre, "but that theory is one of the three accurate ones. Now, Linda's guess: cup number two, willpower is genetic." Pre lifted the second cup, revealing another peppermint plant. "Sorry again, this theory is also accurate. Though I will say that your point about overcoming genetic difficulties is a good one, and we'll come back to it before we're done." Linda looked a bit disappointed, but nodded.

"Finally, Albert thinks the wrong cup could be cup number one, which says willpower never runs out. Let's see if he's onto something." Pre lifted the first cup to reveal several large and live gray-green slugs. A couple of the executives groaned as the slimy creatures began oozing across the table. "I found these little guys in my garden this morning, nibbling on my plants. And, as you've probably guessed by now, Albert was right. The idea that willpower never runs out, that all you have to do when you're tired or stressed or tempted is just try harder, doesn't work."

A few sidelong glances were directed towards Eddie at this, Albert was looking more smug than the rest for his correct choice.

Eddie rolled his eyes. "How the heck was I supposed to know that? I still think working harder is what's going to get us out of this mess."

Pre smiled. "And you're probably not wrong. No matter which willpower paradigm you ascribe to, willpower alone can't replace hard work."

"Wait a minute," said Eddie with a look of astonishment. "Did you just say I was right? Someone call the *Oregonian*, I want this in writing!" The group chuckled, and Pre joined in.

"If there's one thing I've learned, it's when to admit when someone has a good point," said Pre, lifting the remaining cup, that willpower is a day-to-day resource, so the executive could all see that it too concealed a small peppermint plant. "Now that we know the three paradigms that work and the one that doesn't, we can start looking at them more in-depth. I look forward to sharing the inquiry with you in subsequent meetings."

Pre disposed of the slugs, collected the cups and plants and put them back into his bag.

"Now, I would like you to start thinking about the one-on-one sessions we'll do as part of our work together. Each of you, take a few minutes with one or more of the correct willpower paradigms we talked about in mind, and pick the most common or most devastating place where you pull the chicken switch. Write it down if you want. But make sure that it's something truly imperative for you to work on, something that really hurts, not just something that would be nice to fix at some nebulous future point."

A few of the team started scribbling immediately, while others sat thinking.

Pre added, "When you bring your issue to me, I'm going to ask how inclined you really are to solve it. If you can't tell me it's at least an eight or nine on a scale of one to ten, I'll ask you to come back with a different issue."

There was silence for a few minutes as the executives each thoughtfully made notes.

"There are six of you," Pre continued, "So for the next three months I'd like two of you to meet with me each month to work on one willpower issue, a place where you pull the chicken switch. Who'd like to be first?"

"Me," said Roger immediately. "My department has the biggest problem right now. If there's anything I'm doing to contribute to that, I want to fix it, stat."

"I'll go, too," said Trina. "I've got something in mind already that I'd love some guidance on."

"Great," said Pre. "Let's talk on your way out and set up a time to meet this week. Thanks everyone for your attention today. I know the difference you all seek can be obtained here at Trio. Mark, I'll turn the time back over to you."

After some closing remarks, Mark watched as Eddie left the room without so much as a glance in Pre's direction.

Chapter 4: Marshmallows

The sun was barely peeking over the horizon as Roger drove into the trailhead parking lot the next morning. He sipped at a thermos of hot tea and saw Pre's car immediately. It was, to his surprise, the same car Pre drove in high school, a bright blue 1969 Chevrolet El Camino. Pre was stretching and waved when he saw Roger.

"I can't believe you still have that old thing!" Roger called as he got out of his sedan. "Don't tell me it's the same one?"

"Sure is," answered Pre. "She's been repainted and restored a couple times—the moisture up here makes her rust pretty easily—but she's the same beauty she was our senior year."

Roger shook his head admiringly. "That's amazing. I have to tell you, though; I haven't run for a while. This might just be a courtesy jog."

"No worries," said Pre, "We can take it nice and slow. I just like running trails early in the day, it's peaceful and not too crowded."

Roger did a few stretches of his own, then the two men jogged onto the tree-lined trail. They ran at an easy pace for a few minutes before Pre broke the silence.

"So tell me," said Pre, "what's *your* willpower issue? Where is our school valedictorian Roger Coleman pulling the chicken switch?"

Roger laughed. He had been the top scholar of their high school and endured plenty of good-natured ribbing about it.

"Well," Roger said, already breathing heavily, "I've been thinking about that a lot. I think I'm pretty good at leading people. I can teach and train sales techniques, and I can run the sales department well enough. But I wasn't really a great salesperson. I didn't have the persistence. And I think that might be rubbing off on my people."

"You gave up too soon when you were making sales yourself?" asked Pre.

Roger grunted in agreement, saving his breath.

"How about now, do you still give up on things?"

"Honestly? Yeah, I still give up on things, who hasn't?" Roger panted. "I've thought about running for alderman, being on the chamber of commerce, picking up my guitar, or starting to swim again, even going for runs like this regularly, but I give up on most of them when I realize it'll be harder than I thought. I'm about ready to give up on this run, even though I know I could keep going."

Pre chuckled.

"I see it in my group too," continued Roger as they rounded a bend. "I don't have an inside sales manager right now, my last guy quit a month ago, so I'm doing that role on top of my regular work. I have 75 inside sales people, they sell Trio apparel over the phone. These folks try to convince stores to stock and sell our merchandise. But the department close rate is only nine percent. We need to be closer to 30 to turn the profit we want. I think many of them are like me, they aren't very good at turning a no into a yes."

"Why do you say that?" asked Pre, slowing his pace a bit to allow Roger to continue speaking.

"I've listened to dozens and dozens of their calls, maybe hundreds, and most end the same way. The salesperson makes the pitch, the customer says no for one reason or another, and our person ends the call. They give up as soon as they hear no. We've taught sales techniques and lessons on perseverance, but for some reason it isn't sticking and my salespeople, to use your phrase, are pulling the chicken switch. So what you said the other day got me thinking: could my tendency to give up be rubbing off on my salespeople?"

"It's possible," said Pre. "Even if you aren't aware of it, a tendency in a leader might influence the way he or she trains or manages people, and gives the team permission to give up too soon."

Pre thought for a moment. "Let me ask you, how serious is this issue? Scale of one to ten."

Roger drew in a big breath and added, "Before I realized there might be a connection between my issue and my department's issue, I would have said a six, maybe a seven. Now, I think it's a ten. And I'll do whatever you say. Heck, I'm out here running with you, aren't I, even at the risk of being eaten by a Bigfoot?"

Pre laughed. "Good! That's what I like to hear. Now to start solving this issue, I want you to pick one thing that you've given up on in your personal life that you wish you hadn't."

"Would you laugh at me if I said playing guitar?" asked Roger, panting harder. "I used to love playing back in high school. My wife has asked me to pick it up again recently as well as other times over the years. You remember my mom and dad? I know it would make my mom smile to hear me play again."

Pre nodded. "That's a great choice, Roger. How recently have you tried to play?"

"I don't know, maybe last year. I still have my guitar. But do you seriously think me plucking out Jack Johnson songs will help my sales team? I'm no cynic like Eddie, but that seems like a big stretch."

Pre slowed to a walk, letting Roger catch his breath. "Guitar playing, making sales—the activity doesn't matter. The point is to put yourself in a situation where you've been giving up and then to persevere. Remember, the goal is to learn how not to pull the chicken switch—whether you're in an F-16 or not. Make sense?"

Roger nodded, too winded to reply.

"So what we're going to work with is a technique called 'Don't Take the Marshmallow,'" Pre added.

Roger gasped for a breath. "I'm sorry. Did you say *marshmallow*?"

"Yep. It's a lesson I learned from my own time in sales more than twenty years ago. Here's what you are going to do: when we get back to the cars, you are going to stop and buy a bag of marshmallows on your way home. Get the big round ones, the kind you'd take on a campout to make s'mores. Then you will take one marshmallow and put it in a bowl by your guitar. If you spend time practicing guitar later tonight, you get to leave the marshmallow there, but if you don't, you have to eat the marshmallow."

Roger looked confused. "But I like marshmallows! Wouldn't I want to eat it? Like, as a reward for practicing?"

"Oh, the marshmallow is a reward even if you don't eat it. Just a different kind of reward. The next day, if you practice, you add a second marshmallow. The day after, a third. And so on. But if you skip a day's practice, you must eat *all* the marshmallows you've accumulated right then and there, and then you start over again by placing one marshmallow in the bowl. No exceptions. Make sense so far?"

Roger nodded. "Even I wouldn't want to eat six marshmallows at once."

"Exactly," said Pre. "It's a fun and slightly cheesy way to create a chain you don't want to break, and you get used to not pulling the chicken switch when you know you easily could.

"Now any guesses on how I'd like you to bring this idea to your sales team?" added Pre.

Roger thought for a moment: "Maybe I could make ending a sales call *early* the reason to eat the marshmallow. You hang up after the first no and you eat the treat, that type of thing. And whoever has the most marshmallows at the end of a day or week gets some incentive?"

Pre smiled. "Something like that. We can work out the specific details later. But I want you to give yourself two weeks with your guitar practice first. Then, when you start your salespeople on the marshmallow exercise, you'll have an unbroken chain to know it can work. They'll hear the confidence in your voice."

Roger gave a more decisive nod. "I can do that."

"Good," said Pre. "Remember, I'm here to answer questions at any time. And at the next meeting, you'll report to the whole team on how this exercise is going. Sound good?"

"Um, so I'm supposed to report to Mark, Eddie and the rest of the group that I'm playing guitar to improve sales?" asked Roger.

Pre laughed. "Trust me on this; they'll be doing some pretty crazy-sounding stuff too."

"Okay, I'm ready to give it a try—and I'm ready to try jogging back."

The two friends turned began a slow but steady run down the trail.

Chapter 5: Present and Future Self

A couple days later, Trina made the same turn into the trailhead parking lot that Roger had made, at about the same hour of the morning. Like Roger, she was sipping a hot beverage to help herself wake up—in her case it was a latte with extra foam. Unlike Roger, she was somewhat dreading what was about to happen. When Pre had told her and Roger that his training meetings took place on his morning runs, she had put on a brave face and said "Sounds good!" but inside had been pretty uncomfortable.

She parked next to Pre's distinctive blue El Camino. Taking a deep breath, she drained her latte and got out of the car before she could change her mind.

Pre waved at her. "Good morning, Trina! Thanks for meeting me so early."

"You're welcome, Mr. Adams. Um…are we really going to run? How long do you need me to run before we can talk about my issue?"

Pre looked more closely at Trina and realized she seemed pretty nervous. "Please, call me Pre. It's not just Mark and Roger and Eddie, everyone calls me that."

Trina had crossed her arms and looked Pre directly in the eyes. "Look, I'll run if I have to, but…I'm not an athlete, okay? I don't like it much, not since high school."

Pre nodded kindly. "No worries," Pre continued. "We can walk on the trail instead."

Trina let out an audible sigh of relief. "Thank you, Mr. Adams—I mean, Pre. It'll be easier to talk that way, too." The two started down the trail at an easy walk.

"So what's the willpower issue you'd like to work on, Trina? Where are you pulling the chicken switch?" Pre inquired.

"I've got way too much to do," Trina began. "My project list is a mile long, but every time I sit down to work on one of them, another one always interferes. No matter how much work I get done in a day or a week, it's never enough. I have to schedule work two and three months out just to get it on the schedule at all—unless something comes up at the last minute, in which case both it and the work I needed to get done suffer. Plus, since several of the facilities have cut hours or dropped shifts in the last six months, most of my department is as stressed and overworked as I am. I didn't like Eddie's posters much, but I agree with him that I and my staff need the willpower to work harder. Can you help me find it?"

Pre nodded thoughtfully. "Trina, can you tell me how your list gets so long? Other than last-minute fires to put out, how does so much end up on your plate? Are you short-staffed the way Roger is now?"

Trina shook her head. "Not like Roger, no. I'm not missing any major staff roles or managers. It just seems like everything we think will be easy and straightforward isn't, so what seemed manageable when we first took it on becomes impossible once we start working on it. You remember the parking lot renovations I reported on in the exec meeting the other day? Those have been going on for five months. I've received over 50 complaints from employees that they aren't done yet, both because half the lots are under construction and because the other half are still full of potholes. But every time I try to move forward on them, either some other delay comes up with the construction company, or I have to put out a fire, and then another week or two goes by before I get to look at them again. That's just one example. I've got a dozen projects I thought would be easy but are taking forever."

Pre was listening intently. "Okay, I think I understand the situation, but tell me where exactly you're pulling the chicken switch here. Can you identify a particular moment?"

Trina thought for several seconds before answering, "I think it's when I first take on a new project. I know I've got a lot to do, but when Eddie gives me a new project or a new issue comes up, I look at it and think 'Okay, that will be easy, I can deal with it down the line.' Then I say yes when I should say no or not now—only I don't realize I should have said no or not now until it's too late."

"That makes a lot of sense, Trina," said Pre. "It's a much more common issue than you might think. Lots of people deal with this kind of overload issue. It even has a name. It's called the Present Self vs. Future Self Dilemma."

"Okay," said Trina, sounding intrigued. "What does that mean?"

"Your present self is who you are today. You have the schedule, the priorities, and the to-do list that you have right now. Your future self is who you are in a week, a month, or six months. You don't know for sure what your schedule, priorities, or to-do list will be then, so it's easy to assume that you'll have time then that you don't have now. And because the present self is usually so busy, it has an endless supply of optimism that the future self can handle anything that the present self is too busy for. Everything that's impossible now seems possible in the future. Everything we don't have time for now, we believe we'll have time for later. Make sense?"

"I think so," said Trina. "It sounds like you're saying that when I get a new project on my desk, I assume that I'll have time for it later even when I probably won't."

"Exactly," said Pre. "It's easy for the present self to fall victim to the allure of an easy future and then dump a bunch of work on that future without thinking about it. It's not really procrastination, since you're working hard now, but the effect is more or less the same: taking on too much and then wondering why you're so slammed."

Trina was nodding excitedly. "That's me! That's totally what I do! Pre, how do I stop?"

"Tell me one more thing, Trina. How committed are you to tackling this issue and getting it corrected? I guess I am asking, how serious are you? Scale of 1 to 10."

"I'm a 10, Pre. I can't keep going like this. I'll drown by the end of the year. Where do we get started?"

"Three things to start with, replied Pre, "First, every time a new project or task comes across your desk, don't pull the chicken switch and say yes automatically. Take a serious minute to think about how it will impact your future self, not just your present self. Literally, make a note for yourself to take one minute to think every time something new comes up. Developing the courage to take on the present voice in your head first, to not sign up for too much and dump it on the future self, is critical. Second, if after that one minute you know your future self won't be able to handle the project, say no to it or put it into a queue. Third—"

"Wait, wait," Trina broke in. "You know I report to Eddie, right? I can't just tell him no when he comes to me with a project or an assignment. There isn't such a thing as too much work, too many projects, or not responding right now, when Fast Eddie is in charge. You know that's we all call him, because of his impulsive, fast acting, and often over-zealous behavior?"

Pre chuckled. "I know exactly what you mean. Here's how to handle Eddie. Keep a running list of the projects you're currently working on, how much time and personnel you dedicate to each one weekly, how far along they are, etc. When he drops something new on your desk or wants something done faster, show him that list and ask him to prioritize it for you. Make him tell you specifically where to put a task, don't let him just assume you'll make room for it somewhere, and if there's actually no room, show him proof of that. Eddie can be obnoxious and hard headed, but he also lives for getting things done right. A list like that will get his attention in a positive way." Trina had gotten out her phone and was frantically typing notes.

"The third thing I'd like you to do," Pre went on, "is to use what's called the Four Quadrants for Work to organize your task, to-do and project lists."

"Four quadrants, is that like the four cups you showed us? I hope none of them have slugs in them!" said Trina with a shiver.

Pre laughed. "Not quite the same thing. The Four Quadrants is a system based off the teachings of Stephen R. Covey. Have you heard of him?"

"I've heard the name...isn't he the Seven Habits guy?"

"Yes, exactly," said Pre. "Covey is a big name in the field of getting the most important things done, willpower, as well as organization, habit creation, time management, and several other forms of proactive self-help. If you get the chance, I'd recommend looking into his work as a whole. But for your specific issue, we'll start with the Four Quadrants."

"Sounds good, I'll make a note," said Trina, typing again.

"The Four Quadrants concept says that there are four types of actions in your work. Quadrant 1 is work you must do; Quadrant 2 is work you should do; Quadrant 3 is work you're asked to do; and Quadrant 4 is work you shouldn't do."

 "Work you must do, Quadrant 1, is either important work that you and only you can do or supervise, or urgent work that needs immediate attention no matter what. Work you should do, Quadrant 2, is important work that should be done but often gets dropped because it's important, but not urgent, it often involves preparation, prevention, or self-care rather than constant direct productivity. Work you're asked to do, Quadrant 3, is a high priority and urgency, often for someone else, but may not be a high priority for you. Work you shouldn't do, Quadrant 4, is everything else—it's not important for you to do personally, nor is it urgent enough for you to drop other work for it. Make sense?"

Still taking notes on her phone, Trina nodded. "Yes, definitely. So I need to organize my to-do list according to these quadrants? I can do that. Then what?"

"Make sure you assign each new project or task a quadrant number when it comes to you. Then set aside most of your time every day to work on the Quadrant 1 and Quadrant 2 activities. Anything from Quadrant 4, delegate it to your assistant or a manager, someone who can do it for you. You shouldn't find yourself doing Quadrant 4 activities—by definition, they are not your job."

"Now, Quadrant 3 is the tricky one, and where you need to be strongest in not pulling the chicken switch. It's easy to feel obligated when someone asks you to do something for them, even if that task isn't really your job or isn't as high a priority as your Quadrant 1 and 2 tasks. Sometimes you may really need to complete a Quadrant 3 task, if so, complete it and move on. In some cases you may be able to give a Quadrant 3 some time to evaluate before you do anything on it. It might go away on its own, and if it doesn't, you'll be able to respond to it on your own schedule. Still with me?"

"Yes, this sounds great!" Trina enthused, her fingers flying over her phone keyboard. "I can already think of at least five things in Quadrants 3 and 4 that I can pause or get rid of. But won't my getting rid of some of them mean more work for my managers and their employees?"

"Possibly, but let's try this. Put this system in place for two weeks and stick to it. Put your willpower into making the system work.

Then after those two weeks, introduce it to your immediate subordinates and instruct them to try it the way you've been trying it. Then have the rest of your managers implement it. Keep going till your whole department is on the same page. I bet you'll see everyone have more time for what they need to do and drop a whole lot of excess busywork."

"Got it," said Trina, looking up. "Hey, we're back at the trailhead! How far did we walk?"

"A full mile, around one of the shorter trail loops. How did that feel for you?"

"Pretty good! Got time for another loop?"

"Absolutely," said Pre. "Let's try a slow jog this time and see how it goes."

Trina dropped her phone back in her pocket and started walking down the trail with a bit more purpose.

Chapter 6: First Reports

Pre was just stepping out of the elevator, on his way to the next Trio executives' meeting when an angry voice called his name. He turned to see Eddie all but charging toward him, an exasperated Mark and a harried-looking Trina few steps behind.

"Pre, what do you think you're doing? I can't get my own facilities department to do what I want! I don't remember giving you liberty to tell my people how to do their jobs!" Eddie's face was already red and getting redder.

"Fast Eddie, you seem angry," Pre said calmly. "But I seem to remember you being part of the group that agreed to bring me on."

"I must have been out of my mind," Eddie groused. "Whatever you told my facilities manager to do, tell her to quit it! It's ruining everything! My people need to work more, and she's got them working less!"

Mark put a calming hand on Eddie's shoulder, but Eddie shrugged it off. Trina gave Pre a helpless look.

"Alright, tell you what," said Pre. "I'll make you a deal. In this meeting, Trina is scheduled to report on the preliminary results of her work with me, as is Roger. If her results don't meet the approval of the executive team, I'll tell her to go back to how you were doing things before. But if they do, you back off and let her run her department the way that works best for her. Fair enough?"

Eddie glared at Pre for a second, then ground out "Fine." Without another word, he turned and stomped into the conference room.

"I'm so sorry," said Trina. "Your system is working well, but all Eddie sees is that I won't drop everything for him anymore."

"It's fine," said Pre. "Once he starts to recognize the results, he'll come around. I'm glad you stuck it out this month." The three walked into the conference room, where the remaining executives had already assembled and were pouring coffee and juice. Mark strode to the head of the table.

"With the usual morning festivities concluded, I want to start with preliminary reports from Roger and Trina on their work with Pre. Let's hear how things have gone this past month. Roger, why don't you start? I hear there's some, ah, sticky situations down in sales these days." Albert, Lori, and Linda chuckled at this. Roger stood up.

"Well, I got some odd looks when I told my managers that I started practicing guitar again as a way to better understand sales—and some odder ones when I started bringing in marshmallows! But when I explained the idea to all the salespeople and asked for 10 volunteers to try it for a week, I got them right away—and while the average close rate in the department was around 10% that week, those 10 people averaged 17%. The second week we added 10 more, and the 20 averaged 22%! And they're doing it in about 15% fewer calls, because they're staying on calls longer and turning no's into yeses. I'm really happy about where this is going, and I plan to phase in the entire department over the next few weeks. Oh, and I've played guitar all but three days this past month!"

Mark nodded, impressed. "That sounds like a great start. What's your full department closing average now?"

Roger quickly consulted a file he'd brought. "Still low, around 12%, but as more people start the marshmallow system I think that will rise."

Mark nodded. "Anyone have any questions for Roger?"

"How many marshmallows did you have to eat when you skipped practice days?" snickered Lori.

"Three the first time, five the second time, and, ugh, twelve the last time," Roger groaned theatrically. "And that last one was just the longest day, I meant to practice but I didn't even get home until after 10 pm and I just collapsed! Pre, is there any room in this system for emergency days off or anything?"

"Actually, yes," said Pre. "Now that you've followed the system for a month, give yourself one optional day per week. If you have to miss or choose to miss that day, no marshmallows. But if you miss a second day in any week, you must eat three extra marshmallows that day on top of all the others." Roger groaned again, to general laughter.

"It sounds like our sales department is moving in a good direction," said Mark. "Trina, let's hear from you now."

Trina stood, looking tensely between Mark, Pre, and Eddie, the last of whom wouldn't meet her eyes. "Okay, so as you all know I've been focusing on monitoring the amount of work I take on at any given time, and some of my managers are starting to do the same. The bad news is that four projects initially scheduled for this quarter have been pushed back to next quarter." Eddie snorted loudly, and Trina trailed off into silence.

"Eddie, knock it off," said Mark. "Go on, Trina."

Trina took a deep breath and squared her shoulders. "That's the bad news. The good news is that of the remaining facilities projects not pushed back, two are now completed, one will wrap next week, and two of the other five are at least a week ahead of schedule. Two more of those five are either just getting started or are waiting on external factors. All the specifics of those projects are in the agenda for this meeting. Finally, our biggest project, the parking lot renovation, is still getting back on schedule, but as of yesterday's calculations it's now on track to come in at least $20,000 under budget."

Eddie almost fell out of his chair. "What?! You never told me that! That's not possible!"

Trina met her boss's eyes bravely. "You never gave me the chance, Eddie. Every time I tried to explain how things were getting better, you yelled about how I wasn't doing what you had asked. And that reminds me: while I have you and everyone here, I need to tell you that I won't stand for being yelled at anymore. If you need anything from me, please speak to me normally."

Eddie opened his mouth, closed it again, then finally said, "I...alright. If that's what you need to keep delivering progress like that, then you've got it. But I still think we're not working hard enough. Those projects that got postponed are costing us money!"

"Money that we'll make back by working smarter," said Trina. "You've made it very clear you don't like this, but please just see it through. I know it will get even better from here, and I think everyone here will agree and approve, right?" Trina looked around the room, her courage fading a bit.

"I agree," said Roger immediately. Trina gave him a grateful look. The rest of the team echoed his endorsement with nods and smiles at their thoughtful teammate. Eddie sighed and sat back, seeing he was outvoted.

"Alright, Trina. You keep the department moving in this direction, and I'll do my best to let you do it your way. Pre, you win. I'll back off...for now."

"Thanks, Eddie," said Trina, sitting down. "I really appreciate it."

Mark gave her an encouraging smile. "Nice work, Trina. We'll look forward to more good news from you over the next few months. Speaking of that, do you have an estimated finish date for the parking lots now? I know that was a question mark for a while."

Trina opened a file folder of her own. "Now that I've been able to focus on it and keep a closer eye on the contractors, the projected finish date is in approximately six months, which will put us more or less back on schedule. But the first half of the lots will be done within 30-60 days, which will help a lot in getting through the rest."

Mark nodded. "Glad to hear it. Lori, please make sure that info goes out in the company newsletter this week—I know a lot of people will be glad to hear it."

"On it," said Lori, taking notes.

"Okay," said Mark. "I think we're ready for the next part of Pre's training now. Pre, are you good to go?"

"Absolutely," said Pre. "Today we're going to learn more about the first of the four cups."

Chapter 7: Slugs, Curls, and Long Runs

Pre removed one of the red cups from his bag, showed them it was empty, and placed it upside down on the table. The Trio team immediately noticed it now had a large numeral "1" written on it.

"Pre, you're not going to get slug slime all over my nice clean conference table again, are you?" Mark joked as he sat down.

"No, not this time," Pre laughed. "But I did bring a slightly different reminder." He tapped the cup once more, lifted it, and revealed a neon green plastic slug with comically large and floppy antennae. Linda giggled.

"Why slugs?" Pre asked the table at large. "Any ideas why I chose this particular animal to represent the one willpower paradigm from the four I offered that doesn't work?"

"Because they're pretty slimy!" said Trina.

"Because we don't want to be like them?" ventured Albert.

"Because you couldn't afford escargot?" cracked Eddie, apparently recovering his usual sense of humor.

Pre smiled easily. "Albert, you're on the right track again. Look at the characteristics of slugs—they're painfully slow, they leave an icky residue, they're not particularly attractive, they're frustratingly hard to get rid of, and they don't really contribute much. When someone is being lazy or slow, we're even inclined to call them a slug." There were nods around the table.

"Now think about what happens when we don't have any willpower. Without the will to move, we slow down. Without the will to take care of ourselves, our appearance and health deteriorate. Without the will to produce quality work, our production suffers. Without the will to make a positive contribution, we don't contribute much of anything. In other words, when we don't have willpower, we become slugs."

"Okay, I can't argue too much with the slug analogy," interrupted Eddie. "But I still don't see what this has to do with whether people can't just work harder and find more willpower! If you want to get rid of a slug, you just pour salt on the thing and it goes away. If we can't get our people to pick up the pace, maybe we just need to pour some salt on them and the problem goes away. I've pushed through being tired plenty of times and I've seen most people in this room do it too. Heck, I bet you've even done it on some of your insanely long runs!"

Pre nodded. "I have, yes. I've run long races, some as long as a 100 miles, and willpower definitely plays a big role there. But there's a difference between not pulling the chicken switch, and pushing through because you don't believe your willpower will ever run out. One respects your body, the physiological system, and your mind, the psychological system, as well as your capabilities. The other doesn't."

"Wait, what?" asked Eddie. The other executives looked a bit confused as well.

"Eddie, can you come up here a second?" asked Pre. "I've come prepared with an example that illustrates this, and since you brought up the issue, I'd like you to help me demonstrate it."

Eddie hesitated for a moment, but after a few calls of "Come on, Fast Eddie!" from the others, he stood up and walked to stand by Pre. Pre removed a 10-pound dumbbell from his bag and handed it to Eddie.

"Now once upon a time, Fast Eddie, I know you liked to lift weights. So I'm curious, how many times do you think you can curl this dumbbell? It's only ten pounds, so I bet it's a lot. 50 times, maybe? 60? More?"

Eddie hefted the weight. "Ten pounds is nothing! I can curl this puppy at least 100 times."

"Okay, great. Let's see you do it now."

"Wait, why? What do I get if I do?"

Pre reached into the bag again and took out a still-warm Cinnabon. Eddie's mouth started to water.

"Glad you brought that up, Eddie, since once upon a time these were also your favorite snack," said Pre. "If you curl 100 times without stopping, you get the Cinnabon. If not, I get to eat the snack myself in front of you. Sound fair?"

Eddie gave Pre a suspicious look, but nodded. "Okay, tough guy. Get ready to surrender that Cinnabon!" He started curling the weight.

Pre looked around the table. "Roger, will you keep count, please? We're up to four…five…six…" Roger nodded and started writing tally marks on his notepad.

Eddie blew through the first 25 curls without slowing. By 35, he had started breathing a bit harder. At 40, his pace began to drop. The other executives started clapping and cheering him on. Linda even pulled up the *Rocky* soundtrack on her phone and started playing "Eye of the Tiger." Eddie made it to 50, then 55, then 60, as sweat started standing out on his forehead and pooling above his upper lip.

"Come on, Fast Eddie!" called Mark. Eddie grunted with exertion and managed several more reps. Each one was much slower now.

"Now's the time to dig deep, Eddie," said Pre. "Find that willpower!"

Eddie clenched his jaw and slowly curled the weight once…twice…three more times. Then his arm dropped to his side and the weight fell to the floor.

"Crap!" exclaimed Eddie, massaging his bicep. "I thought I could do it! I thought I could just push through. How many was that? 85? 90? At least tell me I was close."

Roger looked up from his notepad. "You only got to 71, Eddie."

Eddie made a disgusted noise and stumped back to his seat. "Fine, Pre, you get the Cinnabon, and I look dumb just like old times. Go on, tell us all what to learn from my failure, we all know you're going to."

Pre smiled at his old friend. "I try not to eat that kind of stuff much anymore. I brought the Cinnabon for you no matter how many reps you did. You tried and you were a good sport about it, so go ahead and take it."

Eddie stared at Pre for a moment, uncomprehending, then leaned across the table and grabbed the Cinnabon. "Thanks, I guess. I still proved your point, though, didn't I?"

"Yes, you did. What Eddie just showed was that no matter how much willpower you think you have, physical energy can run out. If you get to a point where it's gone, you can't just instantly manufacture more. And if you're dealing with a physical or mental struggle, willpower can overcome the limits of your body or mind only up to a point. Beyond that point, either you drop the dumbbell like Eddie did…or you end up hurting yourself. To maximize willpower, you need to be aware of and wisely maintain your physiological and psychological systems."

The room was still again, save for the sounds of Eddie eating his Cinnabon and massaging his fatigued bicep.

"I mentioned earlier that I've run in a number of 100-mile foot races," Pre continued. "What I didn't tell you is that the very first one I ran nearly killed me, or so I thought. Going into the race I felt like Eddie did before he started curling the weight. I'd prepared for years, I'd run enough in training and other races to circle the earth several times, I was mentally and physically ready to go, so I thought. Even the fact that it was pouring rain the day of the race didn't bother me.

"The first 60 miles were fine. They had the usual ups and downs I expected, and I felt like finishing would be very doable. Then my right leg started to hurt a lot. I figured it was just a cramp or just general tiredness, so I ran through it. A few miles later, I tried to refuel at one of the aid stations. I could not force down food. All I could force down was a little chicken broth, nowhere near enough fuel to run 35 more miles. But I was over halfway done, and wasn't willing to stop.

"I had a choice to make, and I made the wrong one. I decided that I was smarter than my body, that I could use willpower to finish the race without proper refueling, rather than dropping out. So I kept running. I did finish the race. I was in agony and I had to literally drag my right leg across the finish line, but I finished. Two days later I was in the hospital. My right leg was swollen to twice its normal size for some reason, blood poisoning or rhabdomyolysis likely. Because I had minimal body fat already at the time *and* had stopped eating to refuel *and* hadn't stopped pushing myself, my body started to cannibalize my muscles as fuel, starting with my right calf. Not only that, but my liver and kidneys needed immediate triage to avoid shutting down. If the race had been 10 miles longer, I shiver to think what might have happened to me. As it was, I was in a wheelchair and on crutches for weeks to rebuild my calf muscle, and struggled with racing for months and months afterward."

The room was silent. Mark and Lori both looked dismayed.

"The good news is," Pre went on, "that I only had to learn that lesson once, and after my recovery I was able to run several more 100-mile races. But I never made the mistake again of trying to unwisely will myself to keep going when my body had nothing left and I don't properly fuel it."

Mark was nodding. "It sounds like what you're saying is that just pushing yourself to have more willpower or work harder is a bit like deciding you are too busy driving to stop and get gas."

"Because no one here's ever done that, right?" joked Linda. Heads turned toward Eddie, who was cramming the last bit of the Cinnabon into his mouth.

"What?" he said, swallowing. "I was trying to get to the cheaper gas station! It was only like four more miles!" The team laughed as the still-grumpy Eddie chased his Cinnabon down with a swig of coffee.

"That's a great way to look at it," said Pre. "In fact, I may use that when we talk about one of the later cups. In the meantime, though, I'd like to wrap up today's talk with a question: what, if anything, is permanent?"

"Twinkies," stated Trina.

"The universe?" asked Mark.

"Death and taxes," said Albert.

"I don't know," said Linda. "Unless we're joking like Trina just was or we're talking about a higher power, I don't think anything is permanent. Everything changes and breaks down eventually."

"I agree," said Pre. "Everything is impermanent—including willpower. So by living in the paradigm that willpower never runs out, we deceive ourselves and, often, we hurt ourselves."

"Okay, okay, I get it," said Eddie. "But tell me this, Mr. Smart Guy Pre. Where does pulling the chicken switch fit into all this? You haven't mentioned it once in the last 10 minutes!"

"Now that," answered Pre, "is a great question. Can anyone tell me what they think the answer is?"

"I have an idea," said Roger after a moment. "When you were running that long race, you thought that quitting was pulling the chicken switch. But really, *not* quitting was pulling it, because you ended up hurting yourself more than if you'd quit. You destroyed the F-16 plane, so to speak. So maybe when you're so focused on unending willpower, you lose perspective. You get confused about what the chicken switch actually is, so you end up pulling it when you think you're not?"

"Yes!" exclaimed Trina. "That makes sense to me, too. When you have an inaccurate perspective, chicken switching looks like perseverance, and vice versa—and we're too stubborn to realize we're going about it backwards. I totally get that!"

Pre smiled at the two executives. "I couldn't have said it better myself."

Linda raised her hand. "Can I meet with you next? I'm chicken switching all over the place these days and I'm ready to get some help!"

"Of course! Meet me by the coffee urn in about two minutes and we'll set it up," said Pre. "Thanks, everyone, for your time and attention today. I'll see you next time."

Chapter 8: Temptation

Two mornings later, Linda drove into the trailhead parking lot and immediately spotted Pre's bright blue El Camino, which Mark had told her about as they chatted after the executive meeting. Pre waved at Linda as she got out of her car.

"You look ready to run this morning," he observed, spotting Linda's hoodie sweatshirt and worn sneakers.

Linda drained the last of her bottle of water. "Some of my girlfriends and I are training for a half-marathon this summer. I doubt I'll be fast enough to keep up with you today, Pre, but easy morning runs have been on the calendar for a few weeks now."

"That's great!" said Pre. "Shall we?" The two jogged easily onto one of the trails.

"So if you're already running most days," Pre said after a few minutes, "I'm guessing that's not the chicken switch issue we will be talking about this morning?"

Linda laughed. "No, not exactly. I've always enjoyed being physically active and my husband and I spend time together doing fun and challenging adventures , so getting more active has been pretty easy for me. The whole preparing for a half marathon thing hasn't been a drag or a pain the way I thought it might be."

"Glad to hear it," said Pre. "So if it isn't running, what is it?"

"It kind of factors into running," Linda began. "I get tempted to eat junk food all the time—and when I say all the time, I mean *all* the time. I can't walk across Trio's campus without stopping to get a cinnamon sugar pretzel from the Auntie Anne's kiosk in the sales wing. I finish dinner with my husband normally around 7:30 and then snack on chips and chocolate until I go to bed at 10:30. I keep a jar of Reese's Pieces on my desk for my employees, but I end up eating most of them myself—and I refill that thing every week! I'm surprised I haven't gained 50 pounds since I started working at Trio!"

"I know the feeling," said Pre. "Especially with those Reese's Pieces—I used to eat them constantly. I'd go to a movie and just inhale a whole package from the concession stand. Have you tried healthier snacks?"

"Tried and failed. I buy them and usually eat a few bites, but then I stop. Either my husband finishes them or they go bad. And the thing is, I can tell I'm starting to get in better shape from all the running, but the other girls in my group seem to be able to sustain the running pace longer than me. I feel like all the junk food is slowing me down. Plus I'm distracted all the time—it's like I can't work or focus for more than a few minutes without stopping to snack. And as if that weren't bad enough, I think my employees are following my lead. Many of them seem to snack a lot, but more than that they also come off distracted and unfocused in many of our meetings. I can already tell that we're not getting as much accomplished as we used to. And the worst part is, I don't feel like I have any control over any of it—it just happens, whether I want it to or not! I am aware on some level I may be using the snacking and distraction it offers to deal with stress or other outside issues."

"Okay, so it sounds like you want to find the willpower to stop eating junk food, that perhaps it's connected to being distracted and either way you want to focus better, lead your employees more strongly, and speed up the process of getting in shape. Do I have that right?"

"Yes, exactly."

"So what's your commitment level on these issues, on a scale between 1 and 10 with 1 being low commitment and 10 being super high commitment?"

"This is a nine, Pre. It's not life-threatening yet, but I can already tell I've let these habits, the unhealthy ones, the distractions, and temptations go on too long, and I especially don't want it to spread any more in Trio."

"Okay, excellent," said Pre. "So first of all, temptation to use unhealthy habits as a coping mechanism is a common willpower issue. The playwright and author Oscar Wilde used to say, 'I can resist everything—except temptation.' And eating junk food is probably one of the easiest temptations to fall victim to. Heck, the stuff is engineered to be addictive and marketed to be irresistible. So there's no shame in feeling tempted to use snacking to cope, or even giving in to the temptation from time to time. That's part of being human." Linda nodded, but kept quiet to conserve her breath.

"The issue is that when we give in to temptation too often, we stop having control over it and it starts controlling us. Before we know it, we're pulling the chicken switch every week, every day, every few hours, or even every few minutes because the temptation has control of our impulses. Does that sound familiar?"

"Yes, absolutely," panted Linda. "It feels almost like that old *Evil Dead* movie sometimes—like my hand has a mind of its own and keeps reaching for the candy jar!"

Pre laughed. "I understand! Now there are two ways to develop willpower to overcome temptation: a physiological way and a psychological way. Any guesses on which works better?"

Linda thought for several moments as they ran. "Hmm, seems like it could be either," she said at length. "I keep going back and forth. Which is it?"

"It's actually a trick question," Pre said with a grin. "When it comes to willpower, physiological practices only work so well on their own, and psychological or mental tactics have their limits as well. The real success comes when you blend the two together and cover both sides. So the right answer is actually 'both!'" Both runners laughed. "So what I'm going to have you do here involves some physical and some mental exercises. The idea is to make sure that neither aspect can undermine or detract from the other one. Make sense?"

Linda nodded and slowed to a walk, pulling out a small notepad and pencil. "We can run more in a minute, but if you've got specifics here I want to write them down."

"No worries. Brownie points for bringing something to take notes with. Now, the two physiological practices I have in mind for you will be fairly easy to start, which will set up the psychological practices to reinforce them. Physiological practice number one: adjust your environment to remove temptation."

"Let me guess," said Linda, "throw out the candy and chips and everything?"

"You got it, and that's just for starters," said Pre. "Let's take it a step further. I want you to make a list of everything else that tempts you or distracts you throughout the day—and then remove or toss as many of them as you can. Since you described your chicken switch as occurring with high frequency, I'd like you to start small and build up your willpower. First, toss out all the undesired foods you can and resist consuming any of those foods for two days. Then make it four more days to resisting, on your way to two full weeks of resisting. Then let's see how focused and purposeful you feel."

Linda scribbled furiously, apparently already making her list. "Okay, I can do that. What's number two?"

"Physiological practice number two is even easier: brush your teeth after dinner."

Linda looked up. "I always brush my teeth before I go to bed, doesn't that count?"

"Actually, no," said Pre. "I mean brush them *right* after dinner, the very minute you get up from the table. That way, when you're tempted to eat any junk food that might become available, you'll be aware that your mouth is all fresh and clean. Salty chips and sticky chocolate will ruin that cool, fresh feeling."

"Ahhhh, I see where you're going with that now, that makes a lot of sense, I'm putting a system in place to assist me in fending off my temptation." said Linda. "I like that idea!"

"I'm glad!" said Pre. "Are you ready for the psychological practices?" Linda nodded again, pen poised. "Okay, the first one is simply to take time to think. Whenever you notice yourself being tempted or distracted, take a moment and think, before you act about why you want to indulge and then, why you want to take back control from the temptation. Be clear that the indulgence will not fix the issue. Then, think about what it is you really want. Maybe it's keeping up with your girlfriends at the half marathon. Maybe it's being a good example for your staff. Maybe it's sharing a healthy life with your husband for the next 50 years. Whatever that 'why' is, make a point of thinking about it for a few seconds every time you catch yourself feeling tempted or distracted. Think about why it's so important to you. I'm not saying this will get rid of the temptation entirely, but it will allow you to stand up to it with more commitment."

"What you're saying makes sense," said Linda. "And I think taking time to think can help with my staff, too. At work, I often get employees in my office that want to jump right into an idea they haven't fully thought through. I'll invite them to sit down and we will flush out the idea together. Often we discover obstacles that make the idea not such a good idea, or we come up with something even better, just by taking time to think things through a bit more."

"Great example," said Pre. "I can see if you are thoughtful, deliberate and focused that way, they will be able to follow you and be less distracted or tempted themselves."

"Okay, I'm almost ready to run again. What's the second psychological practice?"

"It's called priming. Ever heard of it?"

"Like priming a pump to get water or some other action?"

"Yes, sort of. Remember that Auntie Anne's pretzel kiosk you struggle to avoid?"

"Ugh, how could I forget? I don't even like them all that much, I just always end up buying one whenever I go across campus!" Linda shook her head in frustration.

"Did you know that Auntie Anne's kiosks have scent blowers that waft the smell of freshly-baked pretzels up to 100 feet away?"

Linda stopped writing and looked at Pre open-mouthed. "Really?"

Pre nodded. "Mmhmm. If you've ever been walking through an airport or a mall or Trio's campus, and randomly smelled the pretzels, even when you weren't that close to the Auntie Anne's, that's why. Auntie Anne's is priming your 'psychological' pump."

"I have wondered about that a time or two. Is that why I always end up buying one?"

"It's not the only reason, but think about it like this: when you smell a hot, fresh pretzel, you usually start subconsciously thinking about eating that pretzel, even if you weren't planning on it at the time and even if you can't see the pretzel kiosk yet. Then when you walk another 50 feet and the pretzel kiosk comes into view, you're already primed to stop there and buy a pretzel because you were already thinking about it. And even if you don't stop there that time, your subconscious still remembers the pretzel smell and can influence you to stop there later on."

"Aha, so that's how priming works?"

"Pretty much. Priming is the act of influencing your subconscious to want to take a certain action without your conscious mind actually deciding to take it, so that when you do take that action you feel like you didn't actually give it any thought, or even couldn't control yourself. A lot of advertising and marketing out there is designed to do exactly that: prime you to buy their products. Advertisers use all the human senses to prime us. When we are primed by external sources, we can find ourselves pulling all kinds of chicken switches we don't mean to pull."

"That makes sense. I bet billboards are all about priming, aren't they?"

"Absolutely," said Pre. "And priming doesn't just work with advertising. It also works with the general operation of the human mind. Studies have shown that people who think about their grandmothers for a few minutes tend to walk slower right afterwards than people who don't. People who are shown the color yellow are more likely to buy a banana than people shown the color blue. People instructed to unscramble words like 'polite' and 'kind' wait almost twice as long to get an instructor's attention afterwards than those with words like 'interrupt' and 'disturb.' There are dozens of studies on this concept, and they all show that by and large, the human brain can be primed by almost anything to do almost anything under the right conditions."

"Let me guess where you're going with this," said Linda, smiling. "There's some way for me to prime my own brain *not* to buy pretzels and eat junk food every day."

"Exactly!" said Pre. "You know now that the pretzel kiosks and billboards and grocery store displays of the world are already priming you to let them control your buying and eating decisions. So to counter this, prime yourself to control your own decisions first." Linda had begun writing furiously again.

"Here's how I like to suggest people do that," Pre continued, speaking slowly and clearly so Linda's pencil could keep up. "Visualize the outcome you want before you start. If you know you're going to walk across the Trio campus tomorrow afternoon, spend a little time tomorrow morning visualizing yourself walking right past the Auntie Anne's kiosk without stopping. Now I recognize this activity of visualizing is important, but not urgent, therefore it's very easy not to take the minute or two to do it. Don't be that person that doesn't invest the time." Linda nodded again, underlining those words in her notebook.

"You can use priming in lots of situations," Pre went on. "When you're eating dinner, visualize yourself brushing your teeth right after and not eating the rest of the night. When you're making your grocery list, visualize yourself walking through the store and buying only the things on the list.

"When you visualize the actions you want before you start, you're already primed to take them—and that priming allows you to deflect or avoid other potential priming influences that don't align with your best interests. In other words, by committing your willpower to preparation and priming, you don't find yourself defaulting to pulling a chicken switch you didn't want to pull and then wondering why you couldn't stop yourself."

Linda continued writing for several moments, then looked up. "Pre, this is so helpful. I've been feeling like my control has been slipping for weeks now, and now I think there might be a way to get it back. I can't wait to try these practices!"

"I'm so glad to hear it," said Pre. "And I think they will work well for you. Now, are you ready to run some more?"

Linda put away her notebook. "Definitely. Let's get a few miles in before I go throw out my candy jar."

Chapter 9: Genetics and Resources

The executive conference room was buzzing when Pre walked in for the next team meeting. He'd agreed to come during the second half of the meeting this time so the team could get regular business out of the way, and it looked like the team was finishing up their break. Linda was talking excitedly to Albert and Trina, Roger and Lori had their heads together over coffee refills, and Mark and Eddie were exchanging insistent words near the head of the table. The executives looked up and greeted Pre.

"Are we going to hear about the next cup today?" asked Trina. "This one doesn't have more slugs, right?"

"We're actually going to talk about the next two cups today," said Pre. "But first, I'd love to hear thumbnails on how you, Roger, and Linda are doing." Mark looked at Trina and nodded.

"Facilities projects are continuing to move back into schedule and budget, we've actually been able to start one of the projects early that had been moved to next quarter," Trina said. "All but three of the first set of parking lots are finished now."

Roger greeted Pre with a warm handshake. "Inside sales is up to a 15% close rate, now that 35 sales people are riding the marshmallow train. Also, I'm re-learning a jazzy guitar arrangement of Albert Morris's 1974 version of 'Feelings' that I learned back when I was a kid." Everyone in the meeting groaned good naturedly at Roger's revelation regarding his guitar playing.

Linda's smile was even bigger than Roger's. "I haven't eaten a pretzel in a month! My staff meetings are more efficient and productive, too. We're wasting much less time."

Pre gave each of the three executives a fist bump. "Well done, you three. I'm happy to hear things are going so well!"

"Yeah, yeah, that's all great," muttered Eddie. "Marshmallows and schedules and visualizations, oh my. We're really off to see the wizard now." Mark and Roger both glared at their founding partner, who ignored them.

Pre decided to ignore Eddie, taking two red cups labeled 2 and 3 out of his bag. Showing the room they were empty, he placed them upside down on the table. After a moment's thought, he also took out the cup labeled 1 and placed the neon green plastic slug on top of it, winking as he did.

"Now, you may be wondering why I'm bringing up both of these cups in the same meeting," he said. "After all, last time we only talked about one, and this will leave only one left. It's logical that I'd only talk about one at a time, right?" Several team members nodded.

"The reason I'm combining both cups in this meeting is twofold," Pre went on. "The first reason is that while their arguments are different, their solutions are similar. I'll say more about that in a moment. The second reason is that a lot of what I have to say about these two willpower paradigms, at least four of you in this room already know."

Linda, Trina, Roger, and Mark exchanged glances. "You mean, what you've been teaching us so far has to do with these two cups?" ventured Roger.

"Correct," said Pre. "Each of you, tell me what you've learned from our work together so far."

"Clearly, I learned not to take the marshmallow!" replied Roger to general laughter. "And by that I mean the ability to stick to my earlier commitments when things get hard is serving me well."

"I learned to consider my future self when I plan things, not just my present self. To do quality work, I need to be aware of what I commit to," said Trina.

"I learned that by visualizing and preparing ahead of time, I can control my desired positive outcomes rather than letting my temptations control me," answered Linda.

"And I learned that by being aware of the present moment, I can more easily focus on the task at hand and work less distractedly," offered Mark.

"I don't get it," said Albert. "I know I haven't worked with you yet, but I can't see how those lessons learned can all equally relate to your second and third paradigms on willpower. Isn't cup two about genetics, and cup three about resources? How can those four different things be the answers to both cups?"

"Let's see you explain that one, Pre," Eddie called out.

"Don't worry, you will Fast Eddie," said Pre calmly. "Now, Albert raises a good point. Four people, four different solutions to four different chicken switches, none of which have a clear connection to either paradigm two or paradigm three. It certainly could look confusing at first. But let's look at the cups more closely." Pre tapped the cup labeled 2. "The second paradigm says that willpower is genetic, that you're stuck with however much you were given based on your DNA." He tapped the cup labeled 3. "The third paradigm says that willpower is a resource, that once it runs out you can't just keep pushing. Willpower is replenished by physically refueling, through time and sleep or relaxation." He lifted both cups to reveal, once again, small peppermint plants. "Other than both being accurate, what do these two paradigms have in common?"

The executives were silent for several moments. At length Linda raised her hand, and Pre nodded for her to speak. "I feel like they're almost two sides of the same coin," she said. "They're both about the limitations of willpower. One is about genetic limitations and the other is about management of physical resources, but they both deal with some kind of limitation."

"Yeah, I agree with that," said Mark. "The more I think about the two, the more similar they seem even though their basic premises are different." Lori and Roger were nodding as well.

"Excellent," said Pre. "That's what I was hoping you would see. Whether the limits to your willpower come from genetics or from resource management, both paradigms accept that willpower itself is limited. That's the bad news, so to speak. The good news, however, is that from that understanding, people who hold either paradigm can learn and implement strategies and practices to manage the limited willpower they have and create results they didn't think they had enough willpower to create.

"And that's where the four of you come in," Pre continued, gesturing toward Mark, Linda, Trina, and Roger. "The strategies you learned were the solutions to your willpower paradigms, whether you believe that you were born with limited willpower or that you hadn't built up a big enough stockpile of it yet. When I work with the rest of you, the same thing will happen for you. Does that make sense so far?"

"How the hell do you know all this?" asked Eddie before anyone else could respond. "Seriously, how can you possibly tell that marshmallows and visualization and different selves are going to be solutions to limited willpower? I guess I can see giving your willpower time to recharge, that makes sense, but all the rest still sounds like psychobabble to me. Do you have any proof of any of this?"

Roger rounded on Eddie angrily, but Pre held up a calm hand to stop him. "It's a valid question," he said. "And while I could simply point to the progress your four teammates have made so far, I know that won't be enough of an answer for you—in fact, it's rarely been enough of an answer for a sizable percentage of other people I have worked with. So, let me tell you about a few of the resources I've drawn on to design and refine solutions to various willpower issues.

"I mentioned at our first meeting together that I'm not a psychologist, nor do I have a degree in psychology or willpower. I have, however, tested these strategies in the college of hard knocks, meaning my own life. I have tried these practices myself, on myself. I have used these strategies and practices in my own businesses and with the people I have employed as well as those who have hired me to help. Secondly, I have followed closely the work of many psychologists, researchers and scientists over the years who have made it their life's work to study willpower. Some of those studies I've already mentioned to some of you, like the studies on priming that Linda and I talked about and I assume she told you all about in turn." Linda nodded in answer to Pre's implied question.

"Other studies I referred to or even replicated here without even telling you I was doing it. Remember the bicep curls and the Cinnabon last time? That's a variation on a type of study that has shown the limitations of willpower in dozens of contexts. Eddie, tell me something: if I'd offered you the clear choice to eat that Cinnabon or leave it alone after your dumbbell lifting session, rather than just giving it to you, do you think you'd have been able to turn it down—even if you'd been on a strict diet?"

Eddie gave Pre a suspicious look, but eventually said, "Not likely. I was exhausted and frustrated and that Cinnabon smelled amazing."

Pre smiled at his old friend. "Exactly. You'd expended your immediate willpower on one task, that being the dumbbell curls, so you didn't have much left for the next task, that being resisting the

Cinnabon. There have been hundreds of studies like that. Perhaps the most famous one was where half of a group of people were told not to eat some hot, fresh chocolate chip cookies that were placed in front of them, and the other half was told to eat the cookies if they wanted to. Then the whole group individually was asked to solve an unsolvable puzzle. The people who had to resist the cookies gave up on the puzzle long before the ones who didn't.

"Eddie, you also mentioned that recharging your willpower supply makes sense to you, which I'm glad to hear. With you as a former weightlifter, you might be interested to know this idea is actually based on one of the central principles of building muscle: the principle of hypertrophy. Hypertrophy means that muscles don't grow while you're working out, they grow while you're resting and recovering from working out. Willpower works much the same way. Again, this is a tested principle of both fitness and psychology that have been studied in depth for decades.

"Then there is the famous 'Don't Take the Marshmallow' experiment," Pre continued, nodding at Roger. "That is also based on research, specifically a study conducted by Walter Mischel, a professor at the University of Stanford back in the 1960's.

"In that study, a group of five-year-olds were brought into a room one at a time and Mischel placed a marshmallow in front of them. He then told each kid that they could eat the marshmallow if they wanted to, but that if they didn't eat it until he came back, he would give them a second marshmallow and they could eat both. Then he left the room for a couple minutes while his researchers observed the kids through a one-way mirror.

"For some of the children, as soon as he left the room, the temptation was too immense and they ate the marshmallow right away. Other children were able to wait a bit, doing things like poking the marshmallow, licking the marshmallow, but ultimately ate the marshmallow anyway. But some children were able to wait, often by covering their eyes or walking to another part of the room so as not to be tempted by the marshmallow. As promised, these kids got a second marshmallow.

"Mischel was able to follow those same kids through high school graduation and he found some pretty fascinating things. At the time of graduation, many of the same kids that had resisted the marshmallows years earlier had higher grades, more of their own money in the bank, and scored higher on mental aptitude tests then the kids who had not been able to resist the marshmallows." There were audible gasps of surprise from some of the Trio team members at this.

"Now, Mischel controlled the study to make sure that none of the kids came from more or less disciplined homes than the others, and that none of them were hungrier than others. So the study highlighted that for the most part, those kids with a higher propensity for willpower ultimately succeeded more over the next 13 years than those who didn't. But, because the kids were only five, it didn't and couldn't take into account that some of them would learn to manage their willpower, which is why some of the kids who did take the marshmallow ended up doing fairly well by age 18.

"While genetics definitely played a part in this study, Linda's point about nurture vs. nature does play into it as well, and considering that balance ultimately led me not only to some of the similarities between cups two and three, but also to refining the 'Don't Take the Marshmallow' experiment into a challenge to build willpower that works for adults as well as kids—and doesn't take 13 years to prove its results."

Pre held Eddie's gaze for a few more seconds, then looked around the table. "I could go on. There are a number of other studies, research papers, books, and articles I've drawn insight from over the years, and I've had the privilege to meet and interview many of the leading scientists and psychologists in the field of willpower. I can give you a full bibliography, if you'd like."

"No, no, you have made your point," said Mark. The rest of the team chorused agreement—even Eddie looked grudgingly satisfied.

"Alright then," said Pre. "That was a lot of talking from me, and we got through the main point I wanted to make about these two cups, so I'm going to wrap this up here. Eddie, Lori, Albert—who's meeting with me this month?"

"Me, for sure," said Lori. "I've been ready for a couple weeks now."

"I'm in, too," said Albert, a bit sheepishly. "I've been putting it off long enough." Eddie looked at Pre but said nothing.

"Alright then," said Pre. "Let's set it up."

Chapter 10: Procrastination

Albert gave a frustrated growl as he pulled into the trailhead lot close to fifteen minutes after he was scheduled to meet Pre. As he parked, he could see Pre doing burpees at the trailhead. Albert wished for the fourth time that he'd left enough time to get his usual extra-hot coffee, not to mention to arrive on time for this meeting. As Pre jogged back toward him, he gave himself a mental shake and got out of the car.

Pre waved. "Morning, Albert! Did you have some trouble finding this place? I know it's back in the woods a bit."

Albert shook his head, exasperated. "No, I found it just fine. I just didn't leave early enough."

"Understandable," said Pre. "It took me a few months to get used to getting up this early every day, so don't sweat it too much. You ready to run?"

Albert wasn't warmed up, but he didn't want to keep Pre waiting any longer. "Sure, let's go," he said. The two men jogged toward the opening in the trees where the trail began.

"So Albert," Pre asked after a minute or so of running, "what can I help you with? Where does pulling the chicken switch personally show up for you?"

Albert shook his head again. "That's just it, I don't know for sure. I agree with pretty much everything you've been teaching us, and I know I want to have the kind of breakthroughs everyone else is having, but I don't really know where to begin."

"Have you come up with any possible ideas?" asked Pre.

"Sure, a few, but none of them have seemed urgent enough to bother with. You've told my other colleagues that the thing I choose has to be a 9 or a 10 on a 1-10 scale, right? I've got lots of things at five and six, and a couple at seven, but nothing so high as you're looking for."

Pre thought for a moment. "Okay, then let's start with the sevens. Tell me a bit about one of those."

"Well, I think I'll start with what happened this morning. I meant to get here on time, with enough extra time to make coffee first, but I didn't. I even set two extra alarms, but I slept through one and ignored the other for like ten minutes."

"Why do you think that happened?"

"Probably because I didn't sleep enough."

"Why didn't you get enough sleep? Was this meet time a lot earlier than you're used to?"

"No, it wasn't just that," Albert said, thinking harder now. "I didn't get to bed until after midnight. I was cleaning my house till 11:00 and then it took me an hour to get wound down enough to go to bed."

"Not to pry or anything, but why were you cleaning your house so late in the evening?" asked Pre.

"My wife gets home from a business trip this morning," said Albert. "I promised her I'd have the house clean by the time she got back."

"When did she leave?"

"About a week ago."

"So did you not have time to clean during those seven days, did you forget about it, or did you just leave it till the last minute?"

Albert gave a dissatisfied grunt. "I kept putting it off. I had a bunch of work on my plate; however I also watched a bunch of Netflix shows and soccer games, tinkered with my car, shot hoops with some friends, stuff like that. I actually remember thinking 'I need to clean the house' a few times during all that, too. I just never did it."

"Okay, so it sounds like procrastination might be an issue here," said Pre. "Would you agree with that?"

"Sure, I put things off from time to time, but doesn't everyone procrastinate? My staff at times pushes off to-do items I give them, I do the same. And yeah, I lost some sleep over it—and I feel terrible about being late to meet you this morning—but is it really such a big deal or edging on something dangerous? Everything gets done eventually, right?"

"You could say that, but 'eventually' is an unknown specified entity, and some things don't respond well to being left alone or undone for that long, especially when chicken switching is involved."

"See, that's what I'm talking about. I hear what you're saying and I don't disagree, but I still don't see it as so high-priority as to drop everything and change my whole life to fix—ow!" Albert stumbled in mid-step and tumbled to the ground, then sat up clutching his left thigh.

Pre stopped running immediately and crouched in front of him. "Albert, are you okay? What happened?"

"Hamstring...hurts...something pulled...pain," Albert said through gritted teeth.

Pre nodded. "I know how that feels. Sit for a couple minutes, and then I'll help you walk back to the car." Albert nodded, his hands rubbing at the pulled muscle. "I don't have any ice out here or anything," Pre continued, "but I've got a first aid kit in my car with ibuprofen, at least, and I'll drive you somewhere if you need me to."

Albert looked up at Pre and shook his head. "Small…favors…" he groaned. "Automatic transmission…not my…driving leg." He managed a painful laugh.

"Lucky you," said Pre, laughing with him. "I've had to drive my stick shift home with a sprained ankle before. It's not fun."

"I bet," said Albert, now attempting to stretch out the injured leg.

"Looks like you may have pulled your hamstring alright," said Pre. "Will you be okay to walk out of here if I help you? Can you stand up?"

Over the next few minutes, Pre helped Albert to his feet, supported the injured man with a shoulder under his arm and an arm around his waist, they slowly started walking back toward the trailhead. After several steps, Albert shook his head and made a disgusted noise.

"You doing okay?" asked Pre.

"Oh, just peachy," answered Albert. "You know maybe this actually made your point."

"How's that?"

"The other thing I…didn't have time to…do today…was warm up," Albert panted. "I always…stretch before I run…or play hoops or…whatever. Today…I didn't…and look at what happened."

Pre nodded sympathetically. "I know how that feels, too. So if I can ask, how do you feel about procrastination now?"

Albert stopped and turned his head to look at Pre. "You got me. Call it cliché if you have to, but this hurts too much and it's my own fault. I'm a 10 now on that 1-10 scale you always ask about. Let's get this out of my system—and right now."

"Alright, that sounds like a plan," said Pre. "And don't feel like you're alone in wanting to deal with this particular issue—studies show that approximately 95% of people admit to procrastinating, and the other 5% are just procrastinating being truthful about where they procrastinate." Both men laughed. "On top of that, 50% consider themselves chronic procrastinators, lots of them want to stop—they just usually think they'll do it later." The two men laughed again.

"Procrastination is really just putting off a feeling. We associate whatever we need to do with a feeling we don't like, so we choose to feel something more positive instead by putting off the thing until later. Tell me, how do you feel about cleaning the house?"

"I hate it," said Albert, starting to walk a bit more easily as he leaned on Pre. "It's boring, it's drudgery, it's time away from things I want to do, and it always has to be done again a week later. But my wife hates it too, so we take turns."

"And do you both procrastinate on it?"

"You bet we do."

"Makes sense," said Pre. "Now, how do you feel about watching soccer, or shooting hoops with your friends?"

"I love those activities! They're some of my favorite things to do. Soccer's great to watch in season, and I try to make time for a pickup game every week, though I might need to take a week off after today." Albert gave a rueful grin.

"So you hate how it feels to clean, but you love how it feels to watch soccer and play basketball with your buddies. Can you see how you use one to replace or put off the *feeling* of the other?" Albert nodded. "There's your chicken switch," continued Pre. "And it's everyone's who does this. In the moment of needing to do something that feels negative, we choose to do something that makes us feel positive instead. The problem is, we still have to do the negative-feeling thing—and by putting it off, we often make it feel even worse. I hate to say I told you so, Albert, but putting off cleaning your house till last night created all kinds of additional negative feelings for you, as well as undesirable outcomes—you were late, you missed your coffee, you didn't warm up, and now a hurt hamstring. I'm not shaming you for any of this. Do you see the connection?"

Albert nodded. "I see it, don't worry. And you're not going to make me feel any worse about it than I already do. To steal a phrase from Fast Eddie, I feel like a complete dough-dough head."

Pre laughed, startling several nearby birds into sudden flight. "Does he still use that one? I remember it from high school!"

"Sometimes he still does, sure. Lori, Trina, and I always have to bite our tongues until he leaves the room."

"Good to know," said Pre, still grinning. "Now let me ask you something else. When you were *not* cleaning the house these past few days, did you get a lot of work done?"

Albert thought for a second. "Actually, yes. I'm ahead on a couple of tasks that I didn't think I was going to be."

"That's what makes procrastination counterintuitive sometimes," said Pre. "If you keep control of it, you can actually use it to be even more productive than you might be otherwise. Robert Benchley, the American humorist, newspaper columnist and film actor, said it very well decades ago: 'Anyone can do any amount of work, provided it isn't the work he or she is supposed to be doing at that moment.'" This time it was Albert's turn to laugh.

"So Pre," he asked after a few moments, "how do I get on top of this? How do I defend against procrastination?"

"Well, the good news is, you won't actually need to defend against it. Thinking defensively about procrastination tends to put you on the back foot, having to respond to it after the fact when you've already procrastinated and are trying to get things together again. So let's attack rather than defend!"

"Okay then, how do I attack it and from the sound of things, possibly capitalize on it?"

"I've got a few steps for you, and don't worry about writing these down, I'll email them to you later this morning."

"Yeah, I kind of have my hands full right now," joked Albert.

"Yes, you do!" said Pre. "I'm going to suggest six doable steps. Step 1 is Forethought. The first and best way to attack procrastination is to plan ahead. If you go into each day with a plan of when you'll do each task that day—and you stick to that plan—you'll find it easier to overcome procrastination. I'm a big fan of writing it down, so it becomes very real. Doesn't matter if you write it in a planner system or on a piece of paper or sticky note, hell I don't even care if you write it on your hand, but get it written down.

"Step 2 is Prioritize. Do the most important things first whenever possible—even if they're the things that you want to do the least, and even if you think you work well at the last minute. In conjunction with this, I'd also advise to do the thing you hate the most first. Planning for example may not be the most important thing to do, but if it's the task you hate the most, do it first. Willpower is higher first thing in the morning, use it before it gets depleted elsewhere. Next time it's your turn to clean the house, for example, and you've got seven days to do it...do it on day one and get it out of the way.

"Step 3 is Tracking. Keep track of the things you procrastinate on, how you're feeling when you do, what you do instead, and what happens when you do. Use this information to reshape your life.

Now this activity is important, but not urgent, therefore it will be easy to procrastinate taking the time to track this data and the outcomes. Take a stand and track the data.

"Step 4 is called Prime ahead of time. This step helps before a pending task comes up to increase the chances of following through. A good example is that if you plan to go running in the morning, put your running shoes, running outfit and watch in front of your bedroom door before you go to sleep. That way when you wake up, the task of getting your clothes out and ready is already done. You have increased your chances, through priming the situation ahead of time.

"Step 5 is Reward. When you don't procrastinate, when you get tasks done on time, early, or you do things the way you mean to do them, give yourself positive reinforcement. I suggest not using food here, but you could use an episode of your favorite TV show or an afternoon of pickup ball as a reward. I've seen people use massages, hot baths, trips to a bookstore, even date nights with their spouses. Feel free to get creative.

"Finally, Step 6 is Commitment. This is the one that brings all the others together. Without this step, none of the others will work. So make the promise to yourself that you'll do all of these steps, and keep that promise. Be your word. Make sense?"

Albert nodded enthusiastically. "Yes, I'm with you. That's kind of a lot, so I'm glad you'll be emailing it to me, but I think I can do it."

"I know you can. And you don't have to do all six steps at once, either. I suggest starting with the 6th one this week, and making a list of what you're committing to. Then next week, start with step one and make a plan for each day. The third week, add the next one and start doing the most important and hardest things first."

"Okay, I could do that. I'm curious though, why not do it all at once?"

"Well, honestly because trying to do everything all at once can be a recipe for procrastination. The more you try to take on, the easier it becomes to put at least some of it off. There's a sweet spot for the number of tasks or goals a person can effectively take on. Take on too many tasks at once and nothing gets done well. Taking on all the areas of your life where you currently procrastinate is likely too many to tackle all at once. Choose one and correct that one, celebrate and then move on to the next one."

"So starting with cleaning the house first makes good sense?"

"Exactly," said Pre. The two men were coming out of the woods now, and could see their cars in the parking lot only 100 feet or so away. Pre helped Albert to walk the remaining distance to his car.

"You sure you'll be okay to drive out of here?" he asked.

Albert leaned against the car and groaned with relief. "I think so. I'm going to pick up my wife in an hour, so I should have time to get some pain meds into me—and then she can drive us home from the airport."

"Okay, as long as you're sure. I'll email you the steps later this morning. And in the meantime, take care of yourself."

"You got it, Pre. Thanks for getting through to me today."

"You got through to yourself, Albert. And you can keep doing it. Good luck and keep me posted." He watched as Albert drove slowly out of the parking lot, and then turned back to the trail for a long run.

Chapter 11: Speaking Up

Lori surprised Pre when she showed up for their morning run and meeting not in a car, but on her bike.

"Wow, you're really going to get in a workout this morning!" he observed as Lori took off her helmet and locked up her bike.

Lori laughed. "Not quite as much as you think," she replied. "I actually live about a ten-minute ride from here. I'm four times as far from Trio's campus, though, and I still ride there at least a couple days a week. Busy as I am, sometimes it's the only workout I can fit in."

"Good for you for making the time," said Pre. "Ready to run?"

Lori stretched her legs for a few moments, then nodded. "All set."

The two took off down the trail, keeping an easy pace to start. Lori looked over at Pre within the first few steps and asked, "How do you speak up when you don't agree with the people around you?"

Pre gave her a quizzical look. "Is that your chicken switch?"

"It sure is," Lori said. "You know, most of the executive team think that Trina is the reserved one, the one who doesn't speak up or share her opinions as much, who is maybe a little reluctant to disagree. And yeah, because Eddie's on her case so much she's perhaps gone back into her shell a bit, so it makes sense. But if you want to know who's really the anxious or reluctant person on Trio's team, it's not her. It's me."

Pre said nothing, sensing that Lori needed to talk a bit longer.

"Don't get me wrong, I'm good at my job and I know my stuff. When people ask me for my professional opinion, I can give it confidently. But when they don't ask, or when people are just talking in a group, I tend to go along with the crowd. I find myself saying what others want to hear, or what I think they want to hear. I know I'm not telling them what I truly think and feel, I just clam up. Even one-on-one sometimes I'll do that—if the other person has a really strong opinion that I disagree with, I just won't say anything. Afterwards I'll kick myself for it and vow to do better next time, but then I rarely do. Thank goodness Roger's my boss and not Eddie! Roger's not perfect either, but he at least values what I have to say enough to ask for it."

Pre looked thoughtful. "It sounds like you feel like you're not able to be true to yourself in situations where no one is directly letting you know that your opinion is valuable to them. Is that right?"

"Yes, definitely, I often withhold the truth or some of the truth in order to have a sense of being liked, being approved of, or thinking I am easing someone else's situation by withholding." said Lori.

"Is it important to you that other people like you, approve of you, praise you, or give you positive reinforcement?"

Lori was silent for several steps, then replied, "Yes."

"Can you tell me more about that?"

"I...well, um...do you want the whole story?"

"Not if you aren't comfortable with it. How about giving me the 30,000-foot view?"

Lori took a deep breath and slowed to a jog. "Basically, I'm the younger twin. For whatever reason, it always seemed like everyone had good things to say about my sister, and I was always an afterthought."

"So getting people to like or welcome or agree with you, specifically, has been important to you for a while, then."

"Right."

"So would you say that you keep your opinions to yourself so that people will find you more agreeable or think better of you? And that desire ends up being stronger than your desire to share those opinions?"

"Yes, Pre, that's it exactly. There are days I just hang my head in defeat at the number of times I said something that wasn't completely true or I wasn't true to myself, just to feel like part of the group or like people want me around. Please tell me I'm not the only one who struggles with this?"

"Not at all," said Pre. "In fact, I would say that more people struggle with this issue than don't struggle with it. Everyone wants to be liked, included, welcomed, and applauded. Or at least *not* excluded or insulted. Can I tell you a cheesy story about a time I did that myself."

"Please do!" said Lori, relieved.

"I remember in 8th grade, one day after school a group of popular boys in my class cornered me behind the small school we all went to. They all stood around me in a circle and one of them said, 'Adams, I heard today that you like that girly band Duran Duran. But only wusses and pansies like that band. So I wanna know: is it true? Are you a wuss who likes a girly band, or what?'"

Lori looked alarmed. "What did you say?"

"Of course I told them no way! I told them I was into Megadeth and Iron Maiden and Judas Priest like they were. But I bet you've already guessed the truth here?"

"You really did like Duran Duran?"

"Exactly. And I didn't just like them—they were my favorite band! I had posters of them all over my room. I listened to 'The Reflex' at least six times a day. I dreamed about singing on stage with Duran Duran, even though I couldn't really sing. And while I wasn't sure if those kids would beat me up or anything—if it came to that, I knew I could outrun all of them, but I wanted to be liked. So I pulled the chicken switch. I withheld the truth from them. Well, most of them. One of them I eventually did end up telling my secret, but not till later that summer when we started working together on a peppermint farm."

"Wait a second, you mean…"

"Uh-huh. One of those guys was our very own Fast Eddie."

"Oh, boy! How did he take that?" asked Lori, laughing now.

"He laughed at me, of course, and made a few 'Hungry Like The Wolf' jokes, but by that point he and I and Mark and Roger were buddies, so it wasn't that big of a thing. He didn't like me any less, and neither did Roger or Mark.

"Anyway, many of us have the tendency to pull the chicken switch and not be true to ourselves when we want to be accepted, both personally and professionally. Problem is, as you've discovered, when we do that we feel dishonest to ourselves. We feel out of integrity, and can get frustrated—especially if we do it a lot and we feel like we can't stop. In worst case scenarios, false communication like this can cost organizations time and money, and even cost us our relationships. Make sense?"

Lori nodded soberly. "It sure does, Pre. You've got my issue figured out."

"The good news is, like the other chicken switches your colleagues have told me about, this issue can be solved. But before we get into that, can I ask you: how serious are you about solving this chicken switch issue? On a scale between 1 and 10 with 10 being very serious and 1 not serious?"

Lori stopped jogging and faced Pre. "I'm a 10, Pre! I've been doing this for years. I'm not being entirely truthful to my staff, my colleagues, my husband, or myself. I know it won't be easy, but I can't do this anymore. How do I stop?"

Pre put a comforting hand on Lori's shoulder. "You've already started. The first step in stopping pulling a chicken switch is realizing why you're doing it, which you have. Now I do have one piece of bad news for you. Are you ready for it?" Lori nodded, resolute.

"No one is ever going to make you feel valued or accepted unless you value and accept yourself first. There is no reason to be in the business of caring what others think, of needing or wanting to look good or avoid looking bad. All it does is keep you in this frustrated space of chicken switching. So to stop doing it, you need to stop caring what others think of you."

Lori took a deep breath. "That's a lot harder than it sounds. I've tried."

"I know. That's why it's the bad news. But remember the good news: it's not impossible. It can be done. And it starts by understanding that you are not responsible for anyone else's reaction to your opinions. All you are responsible for is being true to yourself, being authentic. If you are being fully authentic and in line with your own truth, what others think of you won't matter.

"I recognize what I'm stating is easy to say and harder to do, but again it's not impossible. Tempered with maturity and wisdom, you can own the responsibility in the communication process with your language. Strive for your language being authentic. That is what you are responsible for. You are not responsible for telling people what they want to hear. You are not responsible for their reactions to what you have to say, especially because you can't control them anyway."

"Are you sure? I do want to share my opinions and truths more openly, but I don't want to hurt people's feelings or be mean."

"Okay, good point," said Pre. "Look at it this way: when your truth is kind and constructive, or at least neutral, prioritize sharing it. If someone disagrees, that's on them. But you're a kind person, so when your truth is unkind, you can still be true to yourself by not sharing it—or at least by doing it tactfully. Make sense?"

"Yes, I think so. This still sounds tough, but I want to give it a try. Can you give me any exercises or practices to help like you gave Roger and the others?"

Pre smiled at her. "Absolutely. The first thing I want you to do is spend the next two weeks getting really aware of every time you pull this particular chicken switch. Make notes of them as they happen, or in a review session at the end of the day. You don't have to make yourself stop or do anything differently yet, unless it feels easy and natural in the moment. For now, focus on noticing the instances *as they happen*. If you want, you can also make notes of what you wanted to say but didn't, and why you chose not to say it. But the first goal is getting into the habit of being very aware. Sound good?"

Lori nodded. "I can definitely do that. I'll get a notebook on my way to work. What else?"

"The second thing is to follow a principle called Be Your Word. The idea of a person's word is usually related to making a promise, like you're giving your word that you'll do something when you said you would. But the root of that is the idea of attaching your personal integrity to that promise, so that the other party would know you'd keep it because you were who you are, not just because you said so. Make sense so far?" Lori nodded again.

"Now, when you follow the principle of Be Your Word, it's kind of a promise for yourself to be authentic, but it's also a sense that whatever you say, your words will represent you. So think about how you want to come across—not how you want others to see you, how you want to *be*—and speak that way. As you work on awareness these first two weeks, be thinking about how to be your word. Then after the two weeks, start with one instance per day where you say exactly what you want to say. After a week of that, move up to two or three times a day. Before long you'll be doing it more often than not."

"Why only once a day? Wouldn't I want to start doing it all the time?"

"You do and you will, but changing something this integral to your true self takes a lot of willpower. Even doing it a couple times at first might feel like putting in a full work day. Expecting yourself to change everything immediately will stretch your willpower too far too fast and lead to more chicken switching. So make sure to start small and easy. You can build up from there in time. Treat this process like a muscle you are exercising, trying to get stronger—the principle of hypertrophy I talked about in the last meeting will help you a lot here."

Lori gave Pre a small smile. "I think I can do that, and I see how it will help. But I'm still a bit nervous about this. What if people react badly? What if they think I'm harsh or disagreeable?"

"Some might. And it can be a struggle when they do, even when you know you aren't responsible for how they feel or what they think. But remember that being true to yourself is the most important thing. There's a quote I love by the sci-fi author Lois McMaster Bujold that says 'Reputation is what other people know about you, but honor is what you know about yourself.' What you're about to do is an exercise in honor, Lori. And I know you can do it."

Lori took a deep breath. "Okay. I'm going to do this. Thank you so much, Pre."

"You're welcome. Are you ready to run a bit more?"

"Absolutely. Let's go!" The two took off down the trail again, Lori with a bit more vigor in her stride.

Chapter 12: Dolphins, Integrity and Belief

"The fourth and final cup," said Pre as he placed the four red cups in a row on the conference table again, "represents the paradigm that willpower is a function of belief and integrity. In other words, willpower is a function of what you believe it is, but it's also a function of your belief in it and in yourself."

"I still think this is way too woo-woo to work," grumped Eddie.

"You're not the first person to say that," Pre answered. "You probably won't be the last. But while I've heard people take this concept really far into spiritual territory, it doesn't have to go in that direction to be effective. Let me start by asking a question, why have you been willing to listen to me?"

"Because we want to turn the company's numbers around by growing our willpower," said Mark.

"Because you're helping us get positive results?" asked Lori.

"Because you do magic tricks and nothing else has worked," bantered Eddie.

"All more or less accurate," said Pre, "but think more about the question. I'm asking each of you to reshape your lives in some way. Make time for this, suffer through that, rearrange something else...my instructions have been hard in many cases! They're a lot of work! They even cause disagreements between you all. It would be way easier to ignore me or to pick and choose a few things I have to say rather than embracing all of it. Yet each of you have been willing to follow my instructions as closely as possible so far. Why?"

The executives were silent. Eddie didn't even have a smart-aleck response this time.

"I'll tell you why," said Pre. "Because on some level, you all believe that the potential results are worth the effort. That's why I've asked each of you to find something that is a 9 or 10 for you, not just a 6 or 7. Because this isn't supposed to be easy. Everything worth working and fighting for will require experiencing pain, challenges, suffering, and setbacks. Every moment of training and developing willpower will drain and tax and test the willpower that you already have. Sometimes that willpower will ebb. Sometimes it will fail outright. But for these issues, these changes, these challenges, each of you have committed to see the experience through. You have decided that giving up is not an option because you believe *not* giving up is worth the price. And most importantly, you have used that choice and that belief to prepare yourselves both physically and psychologically for the challenge.

"One of my favorite stories is from the life of Roald Amundsen. He and his team were the first explorers to reach the South Pole and successfully return. Amundsen spent years fanatically learning and trying things to prepare himself and his teams for polar exploration. During one trip he even experimented with eating raw dolphin meat, just to see if it could be useful as a food source should he and his crew be shipwrecked."

"Dolphin meat? Really?" asked Albert.

"Yep. Amundsen knew that being shipwrecked was a very real potential scenario, and that if it happened, the food he and his team packed could run out. So he made a point of finding out if consuming dolphin meat was an option in order to meet the physical and psychological needs of he and his team. Physically, because he knew that as long as his men had edible food and didn't contract scurvy, they would have the strength to keep going. Psychologically, because he also knew that if they *believed* they had enough food for the trip, they would *believe* their explorations were possible and be less likely to give up in the face of extreme cold, dangers, darkness, storms, and other calamities that may await them."

"Those poor dolphins," murmured Linda.

"Oh please, I bet dolphin is delicious!" put in Eddie. "I've always been a member of PETA—People for the Eating of Tasty Animals!" Linda rolled her eyes.

"Point being," continued Pre, "Amundsen is an example of what you all have been doing these past few months. You decided that accomplishing your goal was worth the price you'd need to pay, and have taken steps to prepare both physically and psychologically to do what you needed to do. And I stress this: I've guided you on specific steps, but you've made the decision and followed through on the commitment.

"This is what the fourth willpower paradigm is about. When you decide that what you need or want to do is worth the price, that goal stops being a task and starts being part of you. So now accomplishing it isn't an assignment, but a matter of integrity. To not do it would take you out of integrity with yourself. And when you approach a task or goal from a place of integrity, your willpower for that task will be there when you need it. Even while you may need to take breaks and recharge, your mind and body will reward you with the willpower you seek in order to achieve what you want."

Roger gave Pre a thoughtful look. "I take it the opposite is also true? If we aren't working with integrity and believing in ourselves to that level, willpower doesn't come easily?"

"Correct," said Pre. "Plus, if our beliefs about ourselves are limiting, our willpower tends to be limited as well. If Amundsen hadn't thoroughly prepared beforehand as well as believed that he would survive the harsh conditions on his way to the South Pole, he wouldn't have had the willpower to complete his journey. Or to paraphrase Henry Ford's words, 'whether you think you can do a thing or not, you're right.' If you believe you are limited by how honest you can be, or if you believe that you can't run as far as others, or if you believe you can't get your work done, or that you are mistreated, or that you can't be as efficient, creative, driven, aggressive as is required, then you are probably right—and trying to come up with willpower to exceed those limits will be very difficult.

"Another way to look at this is with a model called see-do-get. How I see the world is a function of the collective sum total of my experiences in the world. I literally see the world through the lenses of my own experiences. What I see determines what I do. And what I do leads to what I get. Imagine if I believed that no one in the world could be trusted. When I believe that, I see untrustworthy behavior everywhere because my mind is already primed to look for it. When I see that, I make sure I take care of myself first, I avoid connecting too closely with anyone, and I don't believe others when they make promises or commitments. And when I do those things, I likely will become socially withdrawn and a difficult co-worker at best, and flat-out paranoid at worst.

"Now what happens if I, realizing I don't want to be socially withdrawn or hard to work with or paranoid, decide to will myself to be more trusting? How do you think that will work out?"

"It might be tough, but you could totally do that," said Eddie. "You just said that if you want something enough you can find the willpower to make it happen, didn't you? If you want to stop being paranoid badly enough, then go to it."

"I disagree," said Lori.

Eddie did a double-take at the uncommon response from Lori. "What?"

Lori gave Pre a small smile, then said, "I said I disagree, Fast Eddie. I don't think your assessment is right. For one thing, Pre didn't say that works if you wanted it badly enough, he said it works if you're working from a place of integrity. But more importantly, I think that if you try to just will yourself to change your behavior in that kind of situation, it won't work well at all. This is what Pre has been helping us with, reviewing what we believe, so that we behave differently and therefore end up getting different results, hopefully the results we intended."

Pre nodded, smiling proudly at Lori. "You got it, Lori. While you may be able to force different behaviors to get different results, it's far easier in the long run to start with the 'see' part of the model. Change how you see the situation and your potential, which changes what you do, your behavior, which changes what you get, the results. Setting willpower alone against a deeply-held belief is a recipe for futility. Your integrity tells you that the belief is part of you, and so your body and mind treat the willpower like your immune system treats a disease. But if you work within your integrity to change the belief, then you'll find willpower—and positive results—coming more easily."

Eddie threw up his hands. "Fine. Pre you got me again old buddy, me and my big mouth. Congratulations."

Pre gave Eddie a long, level look. "Eddie, do you really believe I'm trying to humiliate you? Or that I'm only here to fix something that's wrong with you?"

"Pre, do you really want me to answer that?" Eddie shot back.

"You can if you want," said Pre. "But bear in mind that you also still need to meet with me about your chicken switch. Everyone else already has, now it's down to you."

"Yeah, yeah. Don't worry, I haven't forgotten." Eddie crossed his arms and looked away from Pre.

"Let's take our break now," said Mark into the following silence. "I know Albert and Lori have Pre reports to share, and then we'll wrap up with a few new business items." The team began standing, some stretching while Pre conferred briefly with Lori and Albert before stepping out.

Chapter 13: Contentions

"...and so what seems to be happening in HR is a lot like what's been happening in the facilities department," Pre heard Albert saying to the group as he slipped back in after the break.

"How so?" asked Mark.

"Well, several tasks that we'd planned for this month or next month have gotten pushed back, and we decided to drop another one altogether. But these things happened because my team is a lot more focused and efficient on what's right in front of us—and on making sure we aren't using the pleasure of complaining about work to avoid actually *doing* the work until we're behind schedule and have to scramble to catch up. We're trying to do fewer things right in the moment, but we're doing those things a lot more effectively."

"Sounds like a good plan," said Trina, smiling broadly at him. Mark and Linda both nodded agreement.

"It's still formative, but it seems like it's working well so far," said Albert. "I've even gotten a couple requests to trade project duties from people. Apparently when I told two of my managers about my wife and I hiring a weekly housecleaner because we both dislike doing it ourselves so much, they put their heads together and realized that they each were doing a few things they disliked but the other one enjoyed. So they figured out a trade." Pre gave Albert a discreet thumbs-up from the back of the room.

"I like what I'm hearing," said Mark. "Is your leg is back to normal?"

"Yes, finally," answered Albert with a rueful grin. "I'm back to shooting hoops every few days—and stretching every time!"

"Excellent," Mark continued. "Lori, you're up. What have you got for us?"

Lori stood up slowly and looked at each executive in turn. "I've talked to a couple of you about this, but not everyone yet, so here goes: my chicken switch was not sharing my thoughts or opinions unless someone directly asked me to. I did this out of fear that you in this room, as well as my staff and even my family, won't like or accept me as much." Several team members looked startled, and both Trina and Albert started to object. Lori smiled but slightly raised her hand to stop them.

"I've realized a few things about that over the last few weeks. The first one is that while I don't think I'll ever stop wanting everyone to like me, I don't have to wait for proof of it like Sally Field getting her Oscar in order to like myself."

"What?" asked Roger. "I think I missed that one."

"Her acceptance speech was mostly her saying 'You like me, you really like me!'" put in Linda.

"Exactly," said Lori. "She'd let herself believe she was overlooked and undervalued for so long that when she won, it seemed like a huge surprise that anyone liked her. Well, I am not going to be Sally Field! I know that most of the people in this room like me, and that most of the people I work with like me, and I'm pretty sure that after eight years my husband likes me, so the first thing I want to report is that I'm working to think of myself as liked and likeable every day." There was a chorus of agreement from the others and Pre gave another quiet thumbs-up.

"The second thing, which builds on the first one, is that even if none of you like me, I can still like myself," Lori continued. "And what's more, I *do* like myself. I may not always get everything right, but I always try to do the right thing, and that's enough for me to start with." There was another general round of nods and affirmations.

"The third and most important thing," said Lori, "is that I'm working on speaking my mind, my opinion, my truth rather than hiding or stifling it, even when it disagrees with the consensus or what my conversation partner may be saying. I even told my husband finally the other night that I wish he would throw out the old jorts he always wears around on weekends! He is not Bart Simpson from 1987!" The team broke up laughing.

"Per Pre's instructions, I'm easing into this a little at a time, so you can expect me to speak up more often in the future—especially if I disagree with something, like I did right before the break."

"Uh-huh," grunted Eddie before anyone else could speak. "That's well and good, Lori, but what does that do for Trio besides make for longer discussions in these meetings?"

Lori gaped at him for a moment. "Excuse me?"

"Everyone so far has brought back results from their departments. I may not like what they're all doing, but I can't much argue with results. Where are yours? Or is this little love-in of yours just going to keep us talking longer every time an issue comes up in here? We waste enough time going back and forth over everything as it is."

Lori's face contorted with anger. "Eddie, shut up! Were you even *listening* to me?"

Roger jumped in. "Fast Eddie, that was out of line even for you. If that was supposed to be a joke, it wasn't funny."

Eddie stood up. "I wasn't joking. Look at all of you! Okay, fine, the company is starting to do better, but look at what we're doing! Eating marshmallows—oh, I'm sorry, *not* eating marshmallows—visualizing our whole days before we even start them, delaying projects, working less, turning down direct orders and disagreeing with direct superiors, and *I'm the only one who sees it!* The cups weren't your real magic trick, Pre, your trick was getting all these smart people I used to respect to start acting so insane!

"And you," he went on, rounding on Mark, "you knew damn well I was against this idea from the start. Just like you knew I was against turning our Trio into a foursome back in high school. But you didn't listen to me then, and clearly you're not listening now." With a last furious look around the room, Eddie turned and walked toward the door.

"Eddie, wait," called Mark. "Come back, please." But the door was already swinging closed.

Chapter 14: Fred

Trio's expansive cafeteria had several alcoves where tables faced large flat screen TVs for employees to watch on their breaks. As it was mid-morning and few Trio employees took early lunch hours, the cafeteria was largely empty. Coming down from the disastrous executive meeting, Eddie had little trouble finding an unoccupied alcove where he wouldn't be easily seen if Mark or Roger came looking for him. Ignoring the TV, which was set to ESPN on low volume, he sipped halfheartedly at a cup of coffee, staring into space while devouring a huge bag of M&M's, his sugar fix of choice when he couldn't get a Cinnabon. His free hand strayed toward his jacket pocket, slipping inside to touch the folded paper it held. After a few moments, Eddie pulled the paper out and read the first few words for the seventh or eighth time.

Dear Eddie,

This isn't working anymore. When we started, there was an "us," but there hasn't been an "us" for months now. You're...

"Excuse me," said a young-sounding male voice. "Is anyone sitting here?"

Eddie looked up to see a clean-cut Trio staff member holding a tray of breakfast food and indicating a seat across the table from Eddie. Eddie shrugged, stuffing the paper back into his pocket. *So much for solitude.*

The younger man sat down and smiled at Eddie. "I'm Fred Ramsay. Shipping and receiving. Just started at Trio last week. Great to meet you!"

Eddie nodded back. "I'm Edward. Operations."

"That's great! Have you been here long?"

"Yeah, you could say that," said Eddie. The last thing he wanted right then was to tell some fresh-faced kid that he ran part of the company.

"That's great," said Fred again, apparently not noticing that Eddie didn't really want to talk. "Everyone I talk to says they've been here for years and they love it. Did you know that Trio's staff turnover is under 50% of the industry average?"

Eddie did know that, but simply said, "Really?"

"Oh yeah. Trio's a great place to work. I've wanted to work here for a couple years now, ever since I did a company analysis of Trio in one of my college classes. It was awesome—I went into that assignment with no idea where I wanted to go after graduating, and it was like the answer just popped up out of nowhere. It was like 'Oh! *Here's* the place for me.' So I pursued every lead I could find that might get me closer to Trio, and just after graduating the shipping and receiving job opened up, and here I am!"

Intrigued in spite of himself, Eddie asked, "What's your degree in?"

"Economics, with a minor in supply chain and facilities management," said Fred. "Shipping and receiving is just the foot in the door for me, or at least I hope so. I'd love to work my way up from there."

"Sounds like a good plan," said Eddie, finding himself drawn to the younger man's excitement. "So what did you learn in that assignment that made you want to work here?"

"Trio does a lot of things right," stated Fred. "Great management, great work place, good business decisions, and the three friends that started this place complement each other's strengths and weaknesses. It's been the perfect storm of success for this place to thrive over the years. I was fascinated to learn about the blood, sweat, and tears that the three founders had to go through in order to get Trio off the ground. The gambles they took with getting manufacturers to make their products is incredible. The fact all three of the guys drained their savings accounts, mortgaged their cars, houses, and everything they had was sensational to learn about. I loved the daring, go-all-in attitude they all shared to make Trio a reality. Something about that story just drew me in, and now it just feels electrifying to be part of the next chapter."

Eddie gave the kid a tight smile. "Sounds like you've done your homework. Glad you're enjoying being here so far." He was about to try thinking of something else to say to this fiery kid who was starting to remind him of his younger self, when a headline on the TV caught his eye: a well-known athlete who had recently gotten in trouble with the law was going to make a public statement.

Fred saw it too. "Hey, can I turn that up for a minute? I'd like to hear this."

Eddie snorted. "If you want, sure. But after what that joker did, I can't believe he'd have much to say that anyone decent would want to hear."

"Why do you say that?" Fred asked.

"You know how respected he used to be! He wasn't just a star, he was the whole sport's golden boy. No one was more dedicated or more disciplined, no one had more willpower or commitment, and no one cared more about service and integrity. He was a family man, a community man, a church man, an honest man. And then this whole other life came out, this dark side that he'd kept secret like Jekyll and Hyde. He's lucky not to be in prison right now! How can he do all these amazing things on the playing field and then choose so poorly in other areas of his life? Where is that guy's integrity? Where is his honor? Where's his willpower to make the choices a rational role model like him should make?"

Fred put down the TV remote and looked curiously at Eddie. "Yeah, he definitely made some mistakes, and I don't agree with a lot of his choices either, but where does it say that just because you're a great athlete that you inherently are great at everything else in your life?"

Eddie gaped at the younger man. "Really? You're taking his side after everything he did?"

"I'm not taking anyone's side," said Fred, "but I'm surprised that it bothers you so much. Haven't you ever made a mistake? Who died and made you judge and jury over him? Just because he worked his butt off, became an amazing athlete and perfected his game, where does it say that means everything else in his life should be perfect?"

"Everyone knows you don't do the stuff he did!" fired back Eddie, feeling his temper rise again. "Everyone thinks he's wrong and a jerk. I'm surprised ESPN is even covering his statement today!"

"Everyone?" asked Fred quietly. "I'll say again, I don't agree with his choices, but people aren't their choices. I'd agree he made some mistakes, but people aren't their mistakes either. And you've mentioned willpower a few times now—just because someone has great willpower in some areas doesn't mean they necessarily have it in all areas, nor does it mean they are not a worthwhile human being.

"Look at the founders of our country—Adams, Jefferson, Hamilton, even Franklin! They were all great men with amazing willpower, and yet they were all flawed. Adams was an angry workaholic, Jefferson a slave owner. Franklin was an absent husband. Hamilton had an affair. Some of these men hated each other. Yet look what they created together. Heck, I bet the three founders of this company aren't perfect either, but look what they've been able to do! Tell me, if you were one of them, do you think you'd be immune to temptation? Do you think you'd be able to say you'd never made a mistake or a bad decision or changed your mind on something? Do you think you'd have the willpower, as you put it, to be perfect in every way?"

Eddie stopped in mid-retort, his anger turning to heavy disappointment. "I was supposed to," he whispered, so quietly that Fred barely could hear him. But before the younger man could say more, the TV picture shifted to the athlete's press conference. Fred quickly turned up the volume.

"...thank you very much," the athlete was saying. "I'm here today to do something that most people in my industry don't do: I'm here to apologize. You all know what I've done and what I'm doing to make amends for it, but I don't want to be one of those athletes who just says 'damn, I got caught' and never acknowledges or expresses true regret for their wrongdoing. So I want to start by saying that I'm not sorry I got caught, I'm sorry for what I did—and more than that, I'm sorry for the person I let myself become in order to do those things.

"Like many professional athletes, I was raised with a strong value system, and like many professional athletes, I lost sight of mine. At some point in my career I just got super arrogant, over-confident and cocky. I became convinced I was invincible, that nothing was outside my scope, that whatever I wanted, it was available to me. I started doing things that were very much against my code of conduct, my value system. And even as I knew I was straying, part of me really wanted that deceptive life. I thought I deserved what I wanted, so I went after it. I believed I was unstoppable, that I would not be caught when my choices began clashing with my value system."

"I became this person that I wasn't raised to be, that I both wanted to be and didn't want to be, and the longer I split myself that way the more trapped I felt by it. I was spending so much time being one person here and another person there that the duplicity started to impact my life. I got careless. I got over-confident. I got cocky. And I got caught.

"To all my fans, assuming there are any left, I say that the intersection of getting caught and my integrity has sparked a series of events that put me in front of the camera right now. I was wrong. I hurt others. I can't take that back. What I can do is clean up the messes I created. I can live my life forward in a fashion that is true, with complete honesty and integrity. To those I hurt, I am sorry. I hope you can forgive me. If not, that's okay. I will still live the balance of my life as a person of integrity, true to my word and my values, from today forward. I'd like to end by thanking those close to me, especially my family and teammates, for their support, and thank you all for listening to me today."

Eddie sat frozen, staring at the screen as the gathering of reporters and observers applauded the athlete heartily. *My God*, he thought. *He could be talking about me. I haven't broken the law or anything, but I know I've felt invincible here in my position, like I can get whatever I want. Is that what I've become—cocky, overconfident, arrogant, believing I'm never wrong? Am I out of control? Am I deceiving myself? Am I acting outside my value system? Have I just not gotten caught yet?* Eddie had heard the saying before, cockiness binds and then it blinds, but never thought of himself as that person. His hand dropped to the folded paper in his pocket again, and his eyes unconsciously turned upward toward the executive conference room. *Maybe today is my getting caught.*

"Are you alright?" Eddie heard Fred ask. His voice sounded several miles away.

Eddie shook his head to clear it, then looked up at Fred, who was now leaning towards him in concern. "Yes, I'm...I'll be fine," he managed. "I've got to go now, though."

"I can walk you back to your office if you want," Fred offered. "You look a little pale."

"No, but thank you," Eddie said. "I...need to be alone for a bit. Look, thanks for the chat. You've given me a lot to think about."

"No problem," said Fred. "I'll look for you down here again sometime."

"You do that," answered Eddie, standing up and turning toward the exit.

Chapter 15: Lifeline

The sun was not yet up when Pre drove his blue El Camino to the trailhead the next morning. The executive meeting had dissolved soon after Eddie had walked out, with Mark attempting to placate a furious Lori and Trina while Roger, Linda, and Albert looked on in stunned silence. Pre had left quietly, half frustrated and half relieved that he hadn't encountered Eddie on his way out. He wondered as he turned into the parking lot if Eddie had actually walked out of the company entirely as well as the executive meeting. *Hopefully not*, he thought. *Even if Fast Eddie can't or won't see it, he IS valuable to Trio. They wouldn't have gotten this far without him. It would be a shame if he left.*

Pre was surprised to see that he wasn't the first car in the lot, as most other runners on this particular trail tended to show up half an hour or so after he did. The other car was a black pickup truck, and someone appeared to be sitting on the lowered tailgate. *Is that…? No way, it couldn't be*, he thought. But it was. As Pre parked and got out, he could clearly see that the man jumping down from the pickup bed was in fact Eddie Rodriguez.

He did not look good. He wore the same clothes he'd had on yesterday, rumpled as though he'd slept in them. His eyes looked bloodshot, his face was smudged, and his normally fastidious hair stuck up in all directions. Even his polished cowboy boots looked scuffed in the hazy predawn light.

"Pre," he rasped, stepping closer to face his old friend.

"Eddie," said Pre quietly.

"I…I think I need some help," said Eddie. "Yesterday morning I found this on the dining room table." His hand came out of his pocket, and Pre could see a piece of paper held in his fingers. It looked like it had been folded and unfolded a couple dozen times.

Eddie held it out to Pre, who took it and began to read by the light of his cell phone.

Dear Eddie,

This isn't working anymore. When we started, there was an "us," but there hasn't been an "us" for months now. You're at work till all hours, then you collapse on your recliner all weekend, only to go back to work and do it all again. I feel like I only see you when you're asleep. Your kids have barely spoken to their father in weeks.

I'm done making excuses for you, Eddie. I know your work means everything to you, but this has to stop. Our kids need their dad, and I need the man I married. Either you figure out a way to be that man again, or we're done.

I'm taking the kids to my sister's for the week. That gives you a few days to figure out what you really want. If you have a plan when we get back, we'll talk about it. If not, well, we won't have much more to talk about.

I love you.

Lisa

Pre looked up. "Lisa. She's your second wife, right?"

Eddie nodded. "I'm her second husband, too. The kids are from her first marriage."

"How old?"

"Mike just turned thirteen. Wants me to call him Miguel, can you believe that? Anna's ten, amazing softball player already. Got an arm like you wouldn't believe. Becca's almost nine. Plays guitar every day, like Roger but without the marshmallows. Great kids."

"When did you and Lisa get married?"

"About three years ago."

"And it sounds like things were good then, but have deteriorated since."

"Yeah," said Eddie sadly. "Sounds a bit like Trio, when you think about it. And that letter isn't all. After I walked out of the meeting yesterday I got an email from Mark, asking me to take the rest of the week off and get my stuff straight. And then I met a young guy in the cafeteria who just started at the company last week, probably 23 years old, who pegged my issues right between the eyes without even knowing they were mine. I'm losing it, Pre. Everything is falling apart."

Pre handed the letter back to Eddie. "I'm sorry to hear it's come to this, Eddie. I want to help. But I need to know what you want. You said some pretty harsh things yesterday to me and to your colleagues. A couple of them wanted your head on a plate, and I wouldn't have blamed them."

Eddie nodded slowly. "I wouldn't either. I've given Trina hell for months, even before you came in. What I said to Lori yesterday was downright cruel, and it wasn't the first time I've said something like that in that room. Mark and Roger barely put up with me and they've known me my whole life. I've turned into an arrogant jerk. I wouldn't blame you if you didn't want to work with me now, either."

"How do you feel about all this?"

"How do you think?" Eddie choked out. "I feel terrible. I screwed everything up again. My life seems like one of using my strengths to the point of overdoing it, so then it turns into a weakness and I screw things up. I screwed up things back when we worked on the peppermint farm, then college, then with my first wife. Damn, I'm such a dough-dough head! And the few people who will put up with me either don't last, or they bring *you* in to try to fix me."

Pre looked at Eddie for a long moment. "I want to ask you something again that I asked you yesterday. Do you really think that I'm here to humiliate you? To 'fix' you? To make you feel badly about yourself so you'd change for everyone else's sake? Do you believe that's why Mark asked me to consult with Trio, and why he and Roger befriended me back in high school?"

Eddie was silent.

"Eddie?" Pre asked gently.

"Yeah, I do," said Eddie softly.

Pre was about to reply when he noticed a few more cars starting to pull into the lot. "Eddie, I have a lot to tell you in response to that, starting with how I had no idea you felt that way, now or then. But let's either sit in my car or walk on the trail while we do it. Okay?"

Eddie saw the cars too. "Okay. We can walk." The two men moved toward the trailhead.

Chapter 16: Stories

"Eddie, I think I owe you an apology," said Pre as they passed the first trees. "I never knew you felt that way about our group, and I never asked. It may sound hard to believe, but I have always admired your zealous nature, your energy and your drive. I never intended you to feel I wanted to change you."

"Then, why does it seem like you have always been on my case?"

"Because I was on everyone's case back then, and to a degree I still am now. It's what I'm good at, and it's served me well in my life and my career. But I see that it didn't make me a very good friend, and I'm sorry for that."

Eddie looked sidelong at him. "You mean that? You weren't just picking on me for being the odd one out of the four?"

"I do mean it. I wasn't then and I'm not now. And I'm so sorry I made it feel that way to you."

"I...okay. Um. Thank you," Eddie stammered. "Apology accepted."

"Thank *you*," said Pre. "Especially for being honest with me about how you felt. Now, I have a question for you."

"Only one?" Eddie attempted a half-hearted joke.

"For now, sure," laughed Pre. "My question is: how long have you had this story?"

"What story?"

"The story that you use your strengths too much and overdo it, that you screw things up, that it's always been this way, that you are a dough-dough head? How long have you thought about yourself that way?"

Eddie thought for a moment. "Honestly, Pre, I can't remember ever *not* thinking that about myself. Maybe when I was a kid and didn't know any better?"

"I see. Now I want to say something that you might not like much. Is that alright?"

"Sure, go for it. I've already gotten enough bad news, a little more won't hurt too much."

"You're right about one thing: you do screw some things up and some people don't want you around right now. But you're wrong about why. You don't screw things up or drive people away because that's your nature or your destiny or just what you always do. You screw things up because you keep telling yourself this story that says you're a screw-up. You drive people away because you keep telling yourself the story that says no one wants you around."

Eddie looked unconvinced. "Are you sure? That sounds circular to me. Why would I tell myself that story if it weren't true? If it causes so much pain?"

"Because it's human nature. We can all be guilty of conjuring up stories about ourselves, about others around us and about our lives that simply are not true. And then we believe those stories we make up and it creates all sorts of behaviors we don't want. We pull the chicken switch when we choose to believe these fabricated stories. You've seen some of that in the last few months. Lori told herself that people wouldn't accept her if she disagreed with them, Albert believed he could procrastinate and never pay for it, Linda believed she was a slave to her sweet tooth, Trina believed she could sign up for unlimited tasks and get them all done.

"And it's not just now. Back when we were all still teenagers, Mark believed that people would find out he was a fake. His story was that he didn't really know what he was doing, and that when everyone found out they'd quit following him or listening to him. And Roger believed he was a geek, unpopular, and unattractive."

Eddie was looking more surprised by the minute. "Really? How do you know that?"

"I know that because they both told me. Separately, and privately, and they asked that I not share that at the time."

"Oh. Okay, I guess that makes sense. What about you, what was your story?"

"My story was that I'd never belong anywhere. I'd known I was going to the Air Force Academy since I was old enough to know what it was, because of who my parents were. But that same family connection kept me isolated from other kids, moving around the world every year or two until I was ten, with parents who weren't around most of the time even after we settled in Oregon. I could barely manage to talk to anyone until I was in middle school. You and Roger and Mark were my first hope that the story might not be true."

Eddie grimaced. "Well, you did belong...but it still seemed like it was at my expense."

"Then let me tell you one more story" said Pre. "It's about a kid I used to know, a kid who could make anyone laugh. He was so good at it that teachers wouldn't even let him talk in class some days. He even got out of a speeding ticket once by making a cop laugh so hard he could barely stand up. And this kid, he worked harder than anyone I've ever seen. Always first to finish moving a line of irrigation pipe when we all were competing against each other, this kid would always be like 'come on guys, let's get to the next field.' Even at sunset he'd say there was time to get one more field done. And you know what else, this kid had a family that loved him. I envied that kid. There's part of me that always will."

Eddie had stopped walking now and looked with vulnerability in his eyes towards Pre. "That's...that's really how you saw me?"

"Absolutely. And I know that Roger envied how likeable you were, and Mark was jealous of how you never pretended to be anything but yourself. I know that Mark and Roger needed the Eddie factor in the mix in order to build the Trio's company that you all have today."

"I want to believe that," said Eddie. "But even if it is true, didn't I already screw everything up again just now? Or over the last few months or years?"

"Maybe you did. But that doesn't make what I just said any less true. Do you remember that story about Steve Prefontaine and the 1972 Olympics?"

Eddie managed a small laugh. "Buddy, I lost count of your Steve Prefontaine stories twenty years ago."

"Okay, fair enough. You remember then that Prefontaine went into the Olympics completely sure that he'd win the 5,000-meter race. But he finished fourth. And he couldn't handle it. He basically flipped out and went into hiding, living in a little trailer on the far end of town, working at a bar, doing whatever it took to stay out of the limelight, not speak to people, and avoided dealing with the fact that he'd lost. His career was over, or at least he was acting like it. But after a while his coach, Bill Bowerman, went to visit him and said something that snapped Prefontaine out of his funk. In the next few years, Prefontaine went on to break most of his own records and have an even stronger career than before. Do you want to know what Bowerman said?"

"Sure, I'd love to," said Eddie.

"So would I," said Pre. "No one actually knows what Bowerman said except himself and Prefontaine. But I have a pretty good guess. I think he said 'Pre, the only thing that happened back there is that you lost. That's it. But just because you lost a race, even a big race like that one, doesn't make you a loser. Only the story you tell yourself can do that.' I think Pre came out of the '72 Olympics telling himself a story that he was a failure, and from his meeting with Bowerman he decided to change the story."

"Here's where I'm going with this, Eddie," continued Pre. "Your life isn't over. You've dug yourself a pretty deep hole, but that doesn't mean you can't climb out, or even that you have to keep digging. Lisa hasn't left yet. Trio hasn't abandoned you. Mark and Roger haven't given up on you, and neither have I. And none of those things *have* to happen! They're not written in the stars or set down on stone tablets somewhere. You can change them…but *only if you change your story*. Acknowledge what happened. Understand why it happened. But don't fall for the story that because it happened, you have messed things up to a point you can't repair them."

Eddie nodded.

"Okay. Now, do you remember when I was talking about willpower coming from integrity?" Eddie nodded again. "That works both positively and negatively. When your integrity is tied up with the wrong stories and you believe negative things about yourself, trying to will yourself to do positive things is hard, while doing negative things doesn't take much willpower at all. That's why you and many others feel like they keep messing things up without trying to—if they believe they always mess up, their willpower naturally flows toward making mistakes or bad choices, no matter how much they try to will themselves not to. When your integrity aligns with positive stories, you don't need to will yourself to do positive things—they come naturally, while negative actions feel like you'd need to force yourself to do them. This is why what stories you tell yourself are so vital."

"So if I tell myself a different story, I can start fixing all this?" Eddie asked hoarsely.

"In a word, yes," said Pre, putting a hand on Eddie's shoulder. "So tell me, if the story that you always screw everything up is not true, what's a different story you can replace it with?"

Eddie thought for a second. "Well, I don't think I should say that I'm amazing and wonderful and never make any mistakes. That sounds like the arrogant jerk I've been playing around the office these last few months."

"I'd agree with that," said Pre. "That story isn't any more real than the one that says you're a failure. What would you say instead?"

"Maybe somewhere in the middle?" asked Eddie.

"Tell me what that would look like."

"Well, um…" Eddie thought some more. "…okay. I'm not perfect. I make mistakes. I'm also a good man! I love my wife and my kids. I love working hard to make my company successful. I love making my friends laugh. And I'm not done living yet. I still have time to be more of the wise man than the flawed man, if I stick to this story every day."

Pre stopped walking and turned to face Eddie. "Now tell me, how important is that you adopt that story on a scale from 1 to 10, with 10 being mission critical?"

For the first time in what seemed like a long time, Eddie smiled. "It's a 13, Pre."

"A 13?" Pre asked, raising an eyebrow.

"Yes, a 13. It's so far above a 10 that even Spinal Tap's 11 isn't high enough. Pre, I have to do this. I have to live this story. I can't go back to being either an arrogant jerk or a hopeless reject all the time. I have to be this man, the man in the middle. He has a chance to make things right—and not just with willpower, but with real integrity."

Pre smiled back and squeezed Eddie's shoulder. "Good. I'm proud of you, Eddie. Now I have one final question."

"Bring it on!" Eddie half-shouted, hope filling his voice. "I'm ready."

"If you were the man in that story, what would you do to make amends for your recent mistakes?"

Eddie gave Pre a decisive look. "Well, the first thing would be..."

Chapter 17: Amends

Four days later

Mark stopped outside the executive conference room and looked back at his two companions. "Are you sure you want to do this?" he asked.

Eddie nodded firmly. "If I don't do it now, we'll spend the next three weeks at each other's throats, and it'll be my fault. I don't know how well this will work, but it will be better than if I don't do anything."

Mark looked at Pre over Eddie's shoulder. "You know what this is about? You're okay with it?"

"I do and I am," said Pre. "I wouldn't support it otherwise."

"Okay," said Mark, shaking his head slightly. "I don't like going into anything blind, and I don't think any of the rest of us will either, but we've trusted you so far, Pre. We'll trust you today."

"I'm glad I've proved worthy of that trust so far," said Pre. He patted Eddie on the back. "Let's do this, Fast Eddie."

Mark opened the door and ushered Pre and Eddie into the conference room, where the remaining executives were already assembled. He immediately knew this was going to be a tough room. Lori and Trina openly glared when Eddie appeared, and the others looked doubtful. Even the normally even-tempered Albert seemed on edge. Mark was trying to think of what to say first when Pre put a hand on his arm.

"First of all," said Pre to the room at large, "I want you all to know that being here right now is not a requirement of working with me, and neither is making any decision or taking any action based on what you're about to hear. I know you're here because I've asked you to be, and I appreciate that you're trusting me right now. I only ask that you listen for a few minutes, and then you are free to respond however you want, or to leave. Is that alright with everyone?"

There were nods around the table, and Pre felt the tension in the room ease just a bit.

"Now, we all remember what happened in this room last week, and several of you have confided in me or Mark that it was both unacceptable on Eddie's part and problematic for the company as a whole. And I know that just having a talk about it today won't change either of those things or solve the issues around them. But I think, if we're willing to approach and talk openly together, there might be a way forward that works for everyone.

"I want to tell you that what you're about to hear doesn't come from me. I didn't try to make it happen or manipulate circumstances in any way. Eddie came to me on his own, asked for help, acknowledged he'd behaved wrongly, and with a little guidance from me, put together a plan for making amends and moving forward. It is my hope that you all will be open to hearing it and make the decisions that feels right to you. Does anyone have any questions or comments before Eddie gets started?"

"Just that it better take about two minutes," said Lori, her voice icy. "Since apparently *wasting our time* is such a big issue in this room."

Before Pre could respond, Eddie stepped forward and faced Lori. His normally coiffed hair was combed into a simple part, and he wore slacks and a pullover sweater rather than his usual suit. "Lori, I had no reason for saying that to you last week. I don't even have a good excuse. I was totally out of line. I'm deeply sorry for hurting you, and for making your moment of celebration all about my own pain. I was wrong to do it, and I will never speak to you like that again."

Lori raised her eyebrows. This was out of character for the typically arrogant Eddie—she'd expected him to brush her off again, as he'd brushed off any reactions to his harsh or mean comments in the past. "Alright," she said after a moment. "I'm listening. I'll hold off on passing judgment until I've heard you out."

"Thank you," Eddie said gently, surprising her again. "I'll try to make it worth your time." Then he turned to the room, taking a moment to meet each executive's eyes.

"Guys..." he began, then stopped, taking a deep breath. "I wanted to say 'friends,'" he went on. "But I don't know that you'd consider me any sort of friend right now. I certainly haven't acted like a friend to any of you recently. We all know that what I said to Lori last week wasn't the first time I've said something that harsh to one of you, not even the first time this year. We all know that I've been pretty full of myself, that I've put being right ahead of being kind— and ahead of the company's success. Over the last few months, I've listened to each of you talk about both personal successes and ways Trio is getting back on its feet, and I've mostly written them off."

"From talking with Pre over the last few days, I've learned that a lot of that behavior was due to my own pain and fear, feeling threatened or ignored or devalued when none of those things were really happening to me. I've learned that I've spent years telling myself stories about who I am and how I have to behave that just aren't true. And I've learned that the results of accepting and listening to those stories have led to a lot of hurtful actions.

"One thing you all don't know is that it hasn't just been in this room or on Trio's campus. Last week, on the very same day as the meeting I walked out of in fact, Lisa gave me an ultimatum. Either I change how I behave with her and the kids, or I lose them." There were audible gasps from several executives at this.

"Some of you know that I got a similar message from my first wife about a decade ago, and I ignored it. Pretty clear what happened after that, right?" Eddie gave a humorless laugh. "What I'm trying to say here is, last week I realized I was being, to use my own favorite phrase, a complete dough-dough head. Again. Or maybe still. And in doing so, I was hurting people I cared about, a company I love, co-workers I respect, and most of all myself. I can't do that anymore. I can't be that person anymore. And I'm going to do whatever it takes to stop."

The Trio team assembled in the room traded thoughtful looks. "Eddie," said Trina, "I'm not going to say I told you so, or even that I'm glad to hear all of this, though both would be accurate. I will say that this sounds a lot different than the Fast Eddie all of us have learned to put up with over the last few years because he's a founder of the company. I like that. But I have to ask you: you do know that you can't just talk your way out of problems you behaved yourself into, right? You're going to have to show us you've changed, that you're not going to go back on all your promises in a week or a month or a year. How can you do that?"

Eddie held Trina's gaze for a moment. "Right now, I can't. Because you're right, there's nothing I can say right now that will show my dedication next week or next month or next year. I have to ask you all to give me a chance to prove with my actions that I am serious.

"I've already taken a first action to prove I'm serious by retaining Pre to coach me one-on-one for the next year. I think we all know that he won't take any BS from me, and I'm confident that by getting in the habit of receiving feedback and guidance from someone who's serious about helping others, it will help me to stop being such an arrogant jerk all the time and start living and working with integrity again.

"I'm also going to give up on my willpower campaign. As fun as the posters could have been, they wouldn't have been true for anyone, including me. I've been acting like I never run out of willpower and that anyone who does is a failure. But the truth is, I've had it backwards the whole time. I *do* run out of willpower. I run out of it all the time. I pull the chicken switch every day—on food, on taking breaks, on daydreaming, on speaking before I think, the list goes on. I just hide it from you all and from myself until I can get home—and then I collapse in my recliner all weekend and ignore my family, which is a big reason Lisa dropped her bomb on me last week. The people I've judged most harshly for running out of willpower, from each of you to famous athletes on TV, are the ones who deserve the most compassion for falling short but getting up to try again. So I want to stop expecting others to do what I can't or won't do, and stop judging them for not meeting standards that I can't meet either. And that starts with doing this."

Eddie took one of his "Rules of Willpower" posters out of his briefcase, unfolded it to its full size, then decisively tore it in half. Roger and Albert clapped briefly, and Eddie grinned at them.

"Next, I am going to stop trying to do everything myself, control everything from my own office, and always be right no matter what. Another thing I've realized is that I've only been considering my own view and ignoring or discounting any others. I want to stop that. If you're willing, I want to ask each of you to meet with me every other week for the next six months. I'd like you to tell me how best I can help you, what I could be doing better, and what you see that I might not be able to see. I especially want to hear where I'm pulling chicken switches that I may not know about." He turned toward Trina. "And you in particular, my amazing, talented, underappreciated facilities manager, I want more input from you. If I'm off track, I want you to be the first to tell me. And I'm making the commitment to not yell or get defensive when you do."

Trina gave her boss a long, considering look, then said, "Alright. I'll give this a try. But if you backslide and start yelling again, I'm walking out of your office then and there."

"Done," said Eddie. He looked at each of the other executives in turn. "Finally, I want to ask each of you, both individually and collectively, to forgive me. I know I've made mistakes and messes here, but I also know that I have a lot more good to bring to Trio, and I want to bring it with your support. It will take time, and I will definitely make more mistakes, but with your help I know I can do it. Mark, will you forgive me?"

Without saying a word, Mark stood up and embraced his friend.

"Roger, will you forgive me?" asked Eddie. Roger nodded and held out his hand. Eddie shook it, then jumped in surprise—Roger had been hiding a marshmallow in his hand! The executives all laughed, including Eddie.

"Linda, will you forgive me?" asked Eddie next.

Linda nodded slowly. "I remember how you were when I started here. I'd like to see you be that guy again. I forgive you."

Eddie turned to Albert. "Albert, will you forgive me?"

"Only if you come and shoot hoops with me this weekend!" replied the HR exec. "If the old Fast Eddie is coming back, you know I need him on the court again."

"You're on!" said Eddie, smiling more widely. "Trina, will you forgive me?"

Trina traded looks with Lori, then shrugged. "I've said I'll give you a chance. If that goes well, we'll talk."

Eddie nodded. "I can work with that. Thank you for giving me that chance." Taking a deep breath, he turned to Lori. "Lori, will you forgive me?"

Lori said nothing for almost a full ten seconds, then shook her head. "I don't know. You hurt me a lot last week, Eddie. I appreciate your apology, but I can't just let that go. I'm not ready for that yet. So I'll vote with Trina on this. You've bought yourself some time to make things right. Once I see how that goes, I'll come back to the question."

"Okay," said Eddie. "I know I have a lot to make up to you. Thank you for letting me try."

Mark stood up again. "Guys, I think we have a workable path forward here. I want to thank Fast Eddie for taking the initiative to come up with it, and for his honesty with us all today. Eddie, is there anything else you want to say?"

"No, that's all from me," said Eddie. "Thanks again, everyone. Now I think Pre has some last comments to share."

"Wait!" called Linda. "What about Lisa and the kids? You said she dropped her bombshell last week…what happened with them?"

"Oh yeah," said Eddie, smiling with just a bit of pride. "That's where I've been the last few days. Lisa took the kids to her sister's in Orange County, so I flew down and surprised them. We spent the weekend at Disneyland and the beach, and I didn't do a lick of work the whole time."

"So things are all fixed?" asked Roger.

"Well, they're not completely fixed yet. But I think we're at 'crisis averted' stage, and Lisa was willing to forgive me after we talked things through. I'm hopeful things will be okay in time, kind of like here."

"I'm glad to hear it," said Mark. "Please keep us posted. Pre, did you have something to finish us up with?"

Pre stepped forward again as Mark and Eddie sat down. "Only this: if we have mutually discovered only one thing over these past few months, it's that when we pull chicken switches, on some level we are deceiving ourselves. Sometimes it's a small deception, sometimes it's a large one. Sometimes it's something we think for a few moments, sometimes it's a belief we've held for years. What each of you has proven is that when you become aware of the deception and stay aware of it from a place of integrity, you can take steps to keep from pulling the chicken switch. You can focus on the present moment like Mark or avoid taking the marshmallow like Roger. You can consider your future self like Trina, take time to visualize the outcome you want like Linda, take proactive steps every day like Albert, and find your truth like Lori. You can even discover that a story you've been telling yourself for years is false and that you want to create a different one, like Eddie. Every day, you have the chance to maintain this awareness and choice, and every day you have the chance to develop your willpower around it. If you do, sooner or later you will find the outcomes you seek.

"The last thing I want to share with you is the summary of everything we've talked through so far, both together in this room and one-on-one on the trail. I call it the seven steps to less chicken switching."

"Why does it always seem like it takes seven steps to fix stuff?" asked Eddie, his voice already noticeably happier. "Seven is too many to remember, I have trouble remember any of my kids seven digit telephone numbers." The team all laughed at this, even Lori.

"I hear you on that," said Pre, laughing as well. "These seven steps are pretty easy to remember because of their sequential nature. Here are the seven steps to less chicken switching:

"Step one is Knowledge. You can't fix an issue until you know what it is. Step two is Desire—if you aren't a 9 or a 10 on desire to identify and work to correct your issues, you'll not likely find the willpower to solve it. Step three is Awareness. This goes deeper than knowledge, it's where you ask yourself the tough questions that help you dig into why you have this problem, why willpower isn't working on it, and what the story behind it is, etc. Step four is Choice.   Each of you has made the choice to take on your issues from a place of integrity, knowing that *not* making the choice is a choice and it's almost always a poor choice. Step five is Commitment. This is backing up your choice with action—not just once, but repeatedly. Step six is Practice. Perfect practice and lots of it makes for achievement of desired outcomes. Step seven is Accountability, where you track your progress or compare notes with a partner or follow a reporting system to make sure you have support.

"The seven steps to less chicken switching is also the final step in our work together. With it, you can revisit any part of what we've done individually or together, you can double down on the issue you're working on now, and you can tackle a new issue that comes up tomorrow. You can apply it to one chicken switch at a time, or multiple ones at once. The seven steps arm you with the power to get back on your feet and rebuild your willpower. Thank you all for your work with me. I sincerely wish each of you, and Trio, the best."

Mark stood again. "Pre, I want to thank you for everything you've shared with us over the last few months. I also want to confirm that while Trio isn't out of the woods yet, this quarter's numbers are showing marked improvement—in fact, they're almost back up to where they were a year ago. I don't think there's any argument that your work hasn't just helped us individually, but has helped Trio when we were worried nothing else could. On behalf of all of us and the entire Trio community, I thank you."

The team began applauding loudly, even Eddie. Pre took a modest bow. "It was my pleasure."

Chapter 18: Epilogue: Race

Three months later

Fred Ramsay was absolutely stoked. Today was a company-wide afternoon off, centered around a party in the newly finished East Parking Lot. The lot had been cleared of cars and set up like a miniature carnival with vendor booths of food and games lining the aisles and picnic tables set up around the edges.

Fred and several co-workers wandered in from the shipping and receiving building, stopping to read a large sign by the main entrance. The sign had a picture of the company's three founders dressed as the Three Musketeers, with a giant heading of "'All For One And One For All' Day!" above their raised swords. At the bottom of the sign was the line "The Big Race—2:00 PM." Fred and his colleagues traded quizzical looks—no one knew what race the sign was talking about, but they'd probably find out soon enough.

As the group lined up to get sausage sandwiches and fried pickles, Fred felt a tap on his shoulder. He turned to see a face he hadn't seen in several months—Edward, the dour-looking older guy he'd talked to in the cafeteria a few months earlier. He didn't look dour now, though. He looked as excited as Fred felt. An attractive woman about Edward's age was holding his left arm, and three kids about Fred's youngest cousins' ages were chattering with them happily.

"Edward, hi!" he said, shaking the man's hand. "I haven't seen you in the cafeteria for a while. How are things?"

Edward, who was wearing running shorts and a white t-shirt, grinned at him. "Never better," he said. "Fred, I'd like you to meet my wife, Lisa."

"It's a pleasure, ma'am," said Fred. Edward's wife smiled widely and shook his hand as well.

"Fred, I've been doing some thinking about what you said when we talked, about wanting to work up through the company," said Edward. "Is that still something you're interested in?"

"Absolutely, Edward. Especially with the growth we've been going through this year, the warehouses getting third shift back, the new marketing campaigns...I'm super excited to be part of Trio's future. Why do you ask?"

"Because I think it's time for you, and other Trio employees to start getting some mentorship to do just that. We old-timers won't be around forever, you know, and I'm starting to enjoy not having to do everything myself anymore. Right, darling?" He winked at his wife.

"That's right—and I'm enjoying it too!" Lisa put in.

"Well, sure," said Fred. "I'm all for learning from you or someone like you. But we're not in the same department, are we? I mean, shipping is part of operations, but only one part. How would it work for you to mentor me?"

"You might be surprised," said Edward. He handed Fred a card. "Come see me first thing next week. We'll talk more about it then. For now, enjoy the party."

"I sure will, thanks!" called Fred as the older man and his family moved off into the next aisle.

One of Fred's colleagues, Greg, clapped him on the shoulder. "Hey, what did the boss man want?"

Fred looked blank. "Boss man? Huh?"

Greg's mouth dropped open. "You mean you don't know who that was? Dude, look at the sign!" He grabbed Fred's arm and turned him to face the Three Musketeers sign once more.

Fred did a double-take. *No way!* he thought. *It couldn't be!* As if in slow motion, he lifted his hand and read the business card he held: *Eddie Rodriguez, Co-Founder and COO, Trio Inc.*

"So what did he want?" asked Greg.

"He…wants to mentor me, I think. I'm supposed to go talk to him next week."

"Wow! I haven't heard of Eddie mentoring anyone before. I didn't even know you knew him!"

"I didn't either," said Fred, still dazed. As Greg and the others moved on to the next booth, he shook his head. *I guess I really did give him something to think about that day.*

About an hour later, a crew began setting up a large Start/Finish banner near the entrance. As Fred and the rest of Trio's employees and their families gathered around, they saw a figure in a white T-shirt climb up on a picnic table with a microphone.

"GOOD AFTERNOON, EVERYONE!" the figure boomed. There were scattered cheers, yells, and applause.

"AS YOU ALL KNOW, TODAY IS A CELEBRATION OF THE IDEA OF ALL FOR ONE AND ONE FOR ALL," the figure continued. "TRIO BEGAN AS A GROUP OF THREE FRIENDS, AND IT NOW CONTINUES AS A COMMUNITY THAT WORKS, SWEATS, AND CELEBRATES TOGETHER!" More cheers.

"MY NAME IS MARK BUCZKOWSKI, AND I WANT TO INTRODUCE MY FOUNDING PARTNERS AND FELLOW MUSKETEERS, ROGER COLEMAN AND EDDIE RODRIQUEZ!" Two more figures climbed up on the table and waved. The crowd cheered louder.

"I ALSO WANT TO BRING UP THE FEARSOME FOURSOME WHO SUPPORT US IN RUNNING THIS GREAT COMPANY—TRINA GOYA,

ALBERT CHENG, LORI KOKOLOV, AND LINDA KIMBER!" Even louder cheers as several hundred people saw their department supervisors climb onto other tables and wave. All seven executives were wearing white T-shirts, Fred could see.

"THANK YOU VERY MUCH!" Mark continued. "I'M ASKING FOR YOUR ATTENTION NOW BECAUSE IT'S JUST ABOUT TIME FOR...THE GREAT RACE!" More applause. "SOME OF YOU MAY BE WONDERING WHAT I'M TALKING ABOUT. WELL, SEVERAL MONTHS AGO, THE SEVEN OF US BEGAN WORKING WITH AN OUTSIDE RESOURCE WHO WAS INSTRUMENTAL IN HELPING US TURN TRIO AROUND. AND ONE OF US, WHO SHALL REMAIN NAMELESS BUT WHOSE INITIALS ARE EDDIE RODRIQUEZ, HAD A BET WITH THIS PERSON THAT INVOLVED GOING ON A RUN." General laughter.

"EDDIE LOST THAT BET, BUT TRIO WON IT—WE GOT THE RESULTS WE NEEDED TO KEEP THIS COMPANY GROWING FOR YEARS TO COME. SO WE DECIDED THAT WE WOULDN'T MAKE EDDIE DO THE RUN BY HIMSELF. WE'D ALL DO IT WITH HIM—ALL FOR ONE AND ONE FOR ALL!" Roars from the crowd.

"AND RACING AGAINST US TODAY IS THAT OUTSIDE RESOURCE I MENTIONED, OUR GOOD FRIEND, STEVEN 'PRE' ADAMS!" Scattered clapping as an eighth figure, this one wearing bright blue shirt, jumped up on another picnic table.

"THE RACE WILL BEGIN IN TWO MINUTES," Mark went on. "IF ANY ONE OF US GETS ALL THE WAY AROUND THE TRIO CAMPUS ONCE BEFORE PRE GETS AROUND TWO TIMES, PRE HAS AGREED TO SIT IN THE DUNK TANK THE REST OF THE AFTERNOON. IF PRE BEATS US ALL, EACH OF US WILL TAKE A TURN. DOES THAT SOUND FAIR TO YOU ALL?" The crowd clapped, stomped, and cheered even louder.

"NOW JUST TO MAKE THIS FUN, THE SEVEN OF US ARE WEARING SPECIAL T-SHIRTS FOR THIS RACE. WE'D LIKE YOU ALL TO CHANT WHAT'S WRITTEN ON THEM WITH US. CAN YOU DO THAT?" The seven Trio executives all turned around so the first few rows could read the backs of their shirts. Pre, almost fell over laughing as a few rows at a time the crowd began chanting "Stop Pre! Stop Pre! Stop Pre!"

"ARE YOU READY FOR A RACE?" called Mark after a minute or so of chanting. Fred thrust his fists in the air and yelled "Yeah!" as loud as he could.

"ON YOUR MARK!" The seven executives and Pre jumped down from the tables and lined up at the Start/Finish line.

"GET SET!" Fred craned his neck to see more clearly, wondering if Mark was going to pass off the mic to someone else or actually do a mic drop.

"GOOOOOOOOOOO!"

As the eight runners began to move at varying paces, Fred felt himself surge forward with the crowd. *I wonder who this Pre guy is,* he thought. *Maybe Eddie can introduce me.* Then all was forgotten in the excitement of the race, the afternoon off, and the beautiful sunny Oregon day.

Chapter 19: Conclusion and Summary of Lessons

Hi, Kit Allowitz here. Thanks so much for reading, *"Don't Pull The Chicken Switch. How to Maximize Willpower and Get Everything You Want Out of Work and Life."* I hope you enjoyed reading the story as much as I enjoyed writing it....I had to use a lot of willpower to get this work completed. It is my hope that you found a few bits of information that might help you with the chicken switches you're pulling in your professional or personal life.

While I was convinced that writing this book in story form would offer an enjoyable and helpful approach in illustrating some insights about willpower, I also wanted to make sure that all of the central lessons in the book got a summary section here at the end. That way, if you didn't catch them all or if you didn't want to interrupt the story to take notes, you could recap them here without having to dig back through each chapter.

So below, broken into three sections, please find brief summaries of each character's chicken switching lesson. Section I includes a few other memorable insights on chicken switching and willpower; along with references should you want to explore these topics more. Additionally you will find in section I, Mark's chicken switching lesson - while I decided to have Mark's meeting with Pre take place before the book started, his lesson does play a part in the plot, so I figured you might like to see it as well. Please know that while these seven lessons are specific to my seven characters, they are not limited to those characters' issues or chicken switches. If any of them appeal to you, feel free to adapt them to your individual situations.

Section II outlines the four cups described by Pre.

Section III details the Seven Steps to less Chicken Switching.

Finally, as a special thank you for reading this book—and a way to kick-start your own willpower journey and stop pulling chicken switches—you can take a free 7-day email course and put the Seven Step system to work for you right away at:
https://www.chickenswitching.com/

Thanks again and enjoy! If you have any questions or are interested in some coaching with your own chicken switches, please connect with me at: kit.allowitz@chickenswitching.com.

Section I

Mark's Lesson: Be Aware Of The Present Moment

- Guiding principle: The human brain is a complex machine that easily gets distracted and can be found thinking about many things at once. This is often called the monkey mind, it can cause challenges to focus and execution of tasks. With awareness and presence, you can teach your brain to focus without using up all your willpower.
- Example: Meditation (by practiced focus on breath, chant, body awareness, feeling or intentionally nothing at all, you can calm your body and mind and find the ability to focus).
- Combats: Distraction, stress, fear/panic, disorganization, shiny object syndrome.
- Increases willpower for: tasks requiring concentration, remaining calm under stress, thinking deeply, maintaining general equilibrium.
- Benefits: Meditation is a natural sort of remedy that soothes many systems in the body. Frustrations go down, energy goes up, distraction and temptation are compacted. Creativity, teach-ability, memory retention, and focus go up. Physiologically, meditation can retard the aging process, lower blood pressure, slow the heart rate, reduce stress and anxiety, provide more energy, cut physical tension, and strengthen the immune system. Psychologically, meditation gets the brain to slow down for a moment or two, calms the thought processes, changes worry into reflection, provides clarity and lucidity, reduces negative thoughts, builds confidence, and helps generate ideas.
- Give it a try:
    o Assignment #1: Ask yourself – do you ever get monkey mind? When does it occur? Is it a problem?
    o Assignment #2: Try mediation for a couple days. Try it for tiny periods of time, even for just one minute

to begin with. Can you sit there, become aware of your breathing, and focus your mind in the way you desire? Does anything feel different after an attentive one-minute try at meditation?
- Resource(s): Secular Buddhism: "Eastern Thought for Western Minds" by Noah Rasheta.

Roger's Lesson: Don't Take The Marshmallow

- <u>Guiding principle</u>: Temptation is a universal human condition and shows up in all sorts of ways. It can be avoided or defeated if the desire is there to do so. By creating a chain of unbroken actions you can fight temptation, use less willpower, and achieve your desired outcomes, whatever those are.
- <u>Example</u>: Marshmallows represent those things we give into that we don't really want (short-term or long-term). Call them temptations. Temptations may not be good or bad, but are things we state we don't really want. Choose to see temptation as marshmallows, treats that perhaps taste good in the moment, but don't serve your long-term goals.
- <u>Combats</u>: Giving up too soon, not following through on daily/regular commitments, lack of determination or self-discipline.
- <u>Increases willpower for</u>: Completing tasks, not giving up, keeping your commitments, practicing something you want to master, learning a hobby, developing a skill, performing repetitive actions, making time for new daily tasks.
- <u>Benefits</u>: Increased confidence both professionally and personally, satisfaction that you beat temptation, finishing long-delayed or difficult tasks.
- <u>Give it a try</u>:
    - Assignment #1: Ask yourself – Is there something professionally or personally that you frequently say yes to that you don't want to say yes to? Convert that temptation into the visual of a marshmallow (or an actual marshmallow, if you want). Now commit to not eat that marshmallow. Give it a try for 1 day. Then 1 week.
- <u>Resource(s)</u>: *"The Marshmallow Test: Mastering Self-Control"* by Walter Mischel.

Trina's Lesson: Signing up for too much – The Present Self vs. the Future Self

- Guiding principle: There is always more to do than time to do it. It's easy in the now to say yes to getting tasks done in the future. We often overcommit without being aware of how it impacts our future. By taking our future selves into account when we make decisions now, we won't inadvertently tax our future willpower before we even get to it.
- Example: Spending time on tasks and activities that are important but not urgent, like exercise, planning, preparing, and building relationships, we can find intense professional and personal satisfaction. Choosing and mastering one goal (like New Year's Resolutions) at a time is wiser than choosing many goals and risking achieving none of them.
- Combats: Over scheduling, overworking, taking on too much, poor time management and planning, feeling like your work never ends, general fatigue/busyness/being overwhelmed.
- Increases willpower for: Goal completion, project management (especially longer, multi-step projects), juggling multiple tasks at once, planning ahead, improving time management, working effectively and efficiently.
- Benefits: Achievement of important and not just urgent activities, less stress and anxiety, better health (both physiologically and psychologically).
- Give it a try:
    - Assignment #1: Take just a moment to observe the next time your present self-signs up for something easily, thus dumping it all on the future self to deal with. Was what you signed up for done in wisdom or in haste? Are you set up to win when your future

self comes face to face with what your past self-signed you up for?
- Resource(s): *"The Willpower Instinct: How Self-Control Works, Why It Matters, and What You Can Do to Get More of It"* by Kelly McGonigal; *"The 7 Habits of Highly Effective People"* by Stephen R. Covey.

Linda's Lesson: Prime Yourself Before You Begin

- <u>Guiding principle</u>: Our brains get subconsciously "primed" to take certain actions by external forces like advertising and habits. We can find ourselves behaving in ways that don't serve our long-term desired outcomes. By purposefully priming ourselves first, we can improve our willpower for taking the actions we want to take.
- <u>Example</u>: Visualizing yourself taking a desired action in the minutes or even hours leading up to when you know you will take it.
- <u>Combats</u>: Impulsive/compulsive behavior (eating, shopping, Facebooking, etc.), bad habits, overspending, low self-confidence/self-esteem.
- <u>Increases willpower for</u>: Changing habits, building discipline and confidence, preparing for challenging situations, leading by example.
- <u>Benefits</u>: Giving yourself space between the stimulus and the response so you can make a thoughtful and helpful decision, fewer impulsive or compulsive actions, and a stronger sense of self-control.
- <u>Give it a try</u>:
    o Assignment #1 – Pick one outcome you are currently getting that you are not pleased with. Make a pre-commitment towards that current outcome now that would help you better achieve the goal you seek. For example, if you plan to work out tomorrow, you could put out your gym clothes the night before. You could spend 10 minutes today preparing for a meeting tomorrow.
- <u>Resource(s)</u>: *"You Are Not So Smart: Why You Have Too Many Friends on Facebook, Why Your Memory Is Mostly Fiction, and 46 Other Ways You're Deluding Yourself"* by David McRaney.

Albert's Lesson: Attack Procrastination

- Guiding principle: Procrastination is human nature. Procrastination is the state of acting against your better judgement. Procrastination is choosing wants over shoulds. Procrastination is decision avoidance. We want to feel different in the moment, so we find something else to do instead of the thing we should be doing. Thinking defensively about this issue puts us on the back foot. Instead preparing for it on purpose allows us to use our willpower proactively rather than reactively and procrastinate less.
- Example: Setting and keeping commitments to do what you say you will do versus succumbing to what feels good in the moment will make facing and solving issues, to-do lists, or other goals achievable.
- Combats: Deeply ingrained habits, procrastination, unconscious tendencies, self-sabotage, self-inflicted missed deadlines and outcomes.
- Increases willpower for: Creating gradual change over time, learning difficult truths about ourselves, sticking to commitments, figuring out systems that work for us.
- Benefits: Fewer inner conflicts, less stress, fewer crises, and less unhealthy impulsiveness.
- Give it a try: Assignment #1 – The very next time you are beset with a should versus a want, just simply choose the should and see how you feel and the outcome.
- Resource(s): *"Willpower: Rediscovering the Greatest Human Strength"* by Roy F. Baumeister and John Tierney.

Lori's Lesson: Being True To Yourself

- <u>Guiding principle</u>: When we truly manage our own actions and behaviors, we live authentically and in integrity to who we really are and what we really want. Our willpower works for us instead of against us.
- <u>Example</u>: Speaking your truth with courage and consideration, even when others may disagree with you.
- <u>Combats</u>: Being out of integrity, fakeness, fear of rejection or exclusion, dependence on the approval of others, being a wallflower, being a yes-person.
- <u>Increases willpower for</u>: Managing yourself and your actions, allowing you to truly lead others from a place of integrity. Standing up for yourself and/or others, building self-love, improving confidence, taking decisive action toward your desires or dreams, asking for what you want or need.
- <u>Benefits</u>: No longer feeling the weight of having to be responsible for what others think, say or how they act. Freedom to share your opinions and truths openly. Increased self-confidence and self-esteem.
- <u>Give it a try</u>:
    o Assignment #1: If you really took a moment to think about it, do you try to look good and avoid looking bad? Why do you do it?
    o Assignment #2: Pick one area in your life you regularly try to look good or try hard to avoid looking bad. For example, if you don't speak up in groups like you'd like to because you fear looking bad, try speaking up, push yourself to speak up and see what happens. Try being true to yourself in that area.
- <u>Resource(s)</u>: *"The Three Laws of Performance: Rewriting the Future of Your Organization and Your Life"* by Steve Zaffron and Dave Logan; *"Leadership and Self-Deception: Getting Out of the Box"* by The Arbinger Institute.

Eddie's Lesson: Challenge the Stories You Create

- <u>Guiding principle</u>: As human beings, we generate stories about ourselves, about others, about the world, and about our perceived reality of the world. Often these stories are not true. By being aware that we generate these stories we can create awareness and then choose to stop the stories, check the stories, or change the stories we tell ourselves that get in the way of maximizing work and our personal lives. We allow our willpower to support positive and beneficial outcomes rather than negative and hurtful ones.
- <u>Example</u>: Instead of saying "I'm not good enough" or "I can't finish this..." or "That boss is out to get me" or "That person is not trustworthy," check that story against reality. Find a realistic and more positive story to tell yourself instead.
- <u>Combats</u>: A lifetime of being run by our stories, frustration, despair, desperation, depression, giving up, believing the worst of ourselves and others, losing hope.
- <u>Increases willpower for</u>: Dealing with tough circumstances, surviving difficult times, committing to long-term personal growth, and/or major changes.
- <u>Benefits</u>: Freedom from stories that may not be true that can impede our life, our work, and our relationships.
- <u>Give it a try</u>:
    o Assignment #1 – Take a couple minutes and ask yourself if there are stories you tell yourself about your life, your work, or your relationships that could be detrimental. Do you? If so – ask yourself how you could challenge those stories and find out what's actually true.
    o Assignment #2 - Now find a trusted colleague or friend and ask them to provide you with an example of a story they see you buying into that perhaps is

> not in your best interest. Discuss with them what you can do about it.

- <u>Resource(s)</u>: *"The Case for Servant Leadership"* by Kent Nelson; *"Triggers: Creating Behavior That Lasts—Becoming the Person You Want to Be"* by Marshall Goldsmith and Mark Reiter.

Section II

The Four Cups (theories) of Willpower

1. Willpower never runs out (FALSE)
2. Willpower is genetic (TRUE)
3. Willpower is a limited resource (TRUE)
4. Willpower is a function of integrity (TRUE)

Cup/Theory One:

Willpower never runs out

This book suggests that this theory is the least productive of the four theories as well as the only one of the four that isn't workable long-term. The belief that willpower never runs out won't work. The body is a machine and it violates natural law to think you can run the machine forever without maintenance, care, and attention.

The most effective strategies to help, if you believe willpower never runs out are the following:

1. Examine, think and eventually alter your paradigms away from this unwise belief that willpower never runs out. History has examples of men and women, professionally and personally who tried to outwit the natural law that you can go forever with no attention to the body as a machine. One example is Robert Scott who competed against Roald Amundsen to be the first explorer to successfully make it to the South Pole and back. Amundsen succeeded while Scott and his entire team froze to death on the South Pole tundra. Don't be one of those people.
2. History is also full of examples of men and women, both professionally and personally, who paid attention to the physiological and psychological systems in order to achieve

amazing results. Examples include business people Bill Gates and Jack Welch as well as triathlon competitor Dave Scott. *Be one of those people.*

3. Aesop, the author who coined many fables, has one about a farmer who owned a goose that laid a single golden egg per day. Growing impatient and wanting more gold, the farmer cut off the head of the goose to get all the golden eggs at once. After the goose was dead, he found not only were there no golden eggs inside, but he had destroyed his golden-egg-laying asset. The same is true about your body. You can't get more than your body can produce each day. If you don't manage your production capability, your body/mind will not be there for you when you need it.

Cup/Theory Two:

Willpower is genetic

Regardless of whether this theory on willpower seems like it applies to you, the challenges of this theory can be strengthened by applying strategies found in this book.

The most effective strategies to help, if you believe you were not born with willpower (or enough of it to resist your temptations) are the following:

1. Recognize we all have our version of the marshmallow temptations.
2. Know that resisting temptation is a choice.
3. Ensure you have safeguards for what temptations you frequently face.

4. Regardless of the intensity of a tempting stimulus and your response to that stimulus, you are endowed with awareness, imagination, integrity, and independent will. You do have a choice.
5. Check in with your desire. Is what you seek truly what you want?
6. Check in with your reason. By that I mean examine underlying issues and your past that can hamper the desired results you seek. Often we have blind spots (things we don't know we don't know) that are at the root cause of pulling chicken switches.
7. Think carefully about how you see and feel towards the temptation. If you take time to look at the way you see and feel things, the way you see and feel things will change. If your desire is high, you can overcome the temptation and not pull the chicken switch.
8. Remember that short-term gratification is not a viable solution or substitute for long-term satisfaction.

Cup/Theory Three:

Willpower is a limited resource

Regardless of whether this theory on willpower seems like it applies to you, the challenges of this theory can be strengthened by applying strategies found in this book.

The most effective strategies to help, if you believe willpower is a limited resource and stopping you from achieving what you want in life are the following:

1. Know that willpower is always available to you as you balance the body and mind's requirement for fuel. Are you properly fueling both systems?
2. Willpower muscles get stronger when you provide rest after stress.
3. Recognize that certain activities and tasks drain willpower, learn what those are for you and act accordingly.
4. Know that there exists a large array of choices that will rejuvenate your willpower reservoirs. Things like food, laughing, commitment, vision, mission, reconnection, rest, and many other things can all re-boost willpower. Find your rejuvenation tools.

Cup/Theory Four

Willpower is a function of integrity

This book suggests theory number four as the most effective mindset for dealing with not pulling the chicken switch in your life. This theory, that willpower is a function of what you believe, combined with wise management of our physiological and psychological systems, provides the believer unlimited potential.

The most effective strategies to help maximize willpower as a function of integrity are the following:

1. Preparation, practice, and building self-control are some of the most important ways to gain access to unlimited willpower reservoirs.
2. Paying attention the physiological and psychological systems that fuel willpower allows access to its unlimited reservoirs.

3. You must continuously be building stronger foundations of willpower; train your body and mind so you can call upon those training habits in times of willpower challenges.
4. Know you must examine your belief about willpower and its components. What are your convictions, stories, theories, and baggage around what is possible and not possible in your life? Take time to look at this, for as you take time to look at things the way you see things can be enlarged towards the belief you need.
5. Realize that if you are not satisfied with the current outcomes you are getting, then the best place to start is with how you see things. As you see things differently, then you will do different things which drive different outcomes.

Section III

The seven steps to less chicken switching.

Willpower is a critical component for organizational and individual effectiveness. Tapping into willpower's full capability allows an organization and its employees to achieve optimal output. Balancing the two ingredients for optimal willpower, the physiological and psychological systems, are the hardest part for any organization and its people to get right.

To achieve the optimal balance between physiological and psychological systems, an organization and its employees need to follow a sequential examination process so as to carefully choose what to go after, insure they acquire knowledge, desire, create awareness, identify their choices, gain commitment, and are willing to practice and establish an accountability system before using willpower to pursue desired outcomes. When this seven step process is worked through, you can get everything you want out of work and life.

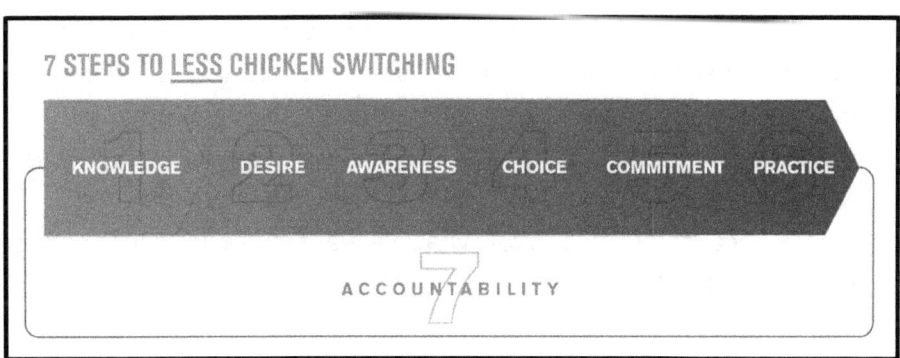

Step One – Knowledge.

Gain knowledge

Get knowledgeable about your desired outcome. Do research. What is required? Be well-informed. Get information about what you are potentially taking on as a goal, the desired outcome, or saying yes to. Knowledge gives you power. Do you understand fully or at least enough to later make a well informed decision about what you want when the temptations come. For example, if you want to lose weight, have you really taken the time to understand the science behind weight loss? Do you understand it enough to develop a well-informed plan? Do you understand why most fail at weight loss in the long run? What do those who succeed do differently?

Step Two – Desire.

Detect desire

Is desire really there for what you say you want? Do you really want this? Is it something you desire or is this something else others want for you? Are you pursuing this for reasons other than authentic reasons? An example, why are you losing weight? Is your desire to lose weight going to sustain itself when temptation and procrastination come calling? Is your desire strong enough so when the alarm rings early in the morning, you will get your back off the bed and get up and exercise? Often goals fizzle and willpower weans because our desire for what we want isn't truly there or has been fabricated by others.

Step Three – Awareness.

Create awareness

Awareness is a deeper cut of knowledge. Taking the time to think through some or all of the following perspectives will help insure you are going after what you want. Questions like: Have I taken the time to really stand apart from what I think I know, from how the world occurs to me, to insure I am potentially taking on this desired outcome with my eyes wide open? Am I aware of where challenges will arise? Am I aware of where my willpower will be challenged? Am I aware of how my mind will respond when things get tough, when temptation and adversity show up? Am I seeing what I want clearly? Am I doing it for reasons I want versus what others may want? Is that good or bad? Does any of this matter to me?

Step Four – Choice.

Choose choice

Creating awareness, checking in on desire, and acquiring knowledge sets you up to make a well informed decision. We call this a choice. A choice that will more likely stand up against the temptation, the triggers, the stimuli that will come in the pursuit of a goal or desired outcome. The pursuit of your goal will most certainly come under heavy fire from the realities of life and forces that push against you reaching what you desire. Without a strong awareness, desire and knowledge, the statistics say you will more likely choose to abandon your goal before completion.

Spending a little time thinking about your goal, rather than just jumping in and haphazardly committing, significantly increases the chances of combating the forces that oppose you reaching your goal. It's important to note that regardless of how much current fortitude you have behind your goal, once you choose it, you have also birthed the seed for the chicken switch. You have also created a situation where you will face pressure to cave, as well as the risk of your willpower reservoir flood gates busting open, draining all that willpower rapidly. Trouble could loom, are you ready?

Step Five – Commitment.

Make commitment

With knowledge, desire, awareness, and authentic choice under your belt, you are poised to make a commitment that has teeth to it, that keeps a lid on trouble you can't handle. Following this sequence is much more empirically sound. You are signing up for something that you have really thought about, rather than randomly jumped into.

Commitment is the culmination of knowledge, desire, awareness, and choice into a vocal, visual, audible statement, a promise, pledge, and vow that you intend to begin. Commitment then becomes your word. It becomes your promise. It becomes now a matter of your integrity; will you follow through on your promise(s) after the emotion of making the promise has passed. This step, commingled with the others, is the glue that holds the model together and makes goal achievement possible. Commitment trumps willpower. Commitment trumps perseverance. Commitment trumps drive. Commitment trumps performance. Commitment trumps successes. Commitment trumps the machine. Commitment is your word. To become very steadfast to the commitments you make is a very strong step to fend off pulling the chicken switch.

Step Six – Practice.

Do practice

Practice is where commitment takes flight. Practice becomes the action to your commitment. Whether you are taking on a difficult assignment at work, facing a tough employee or boss, losing weight, learning to play the guitar, quitting smoking, no longer gossiping, or getting to the gym, practice is what turns your knowledge, desire, and commitment into the germination of the eventual desired outcome. Whatever mechanisms speak your language, you must use them to activate practice in your life related to the desired outcome you seek. Practice, practice, and more practice.

These first 6 steps take a person from origination of what you want through knowing about what you want and insure you have authentic desire, strong awareness and choice in order to make a commitment and then practice what it is you are seeking as a desired outcome. The sequential set of steps allows for the best possible defense against temptation and weaning willpower along the way.

Warning: These six steps are all of a proactive nature. This means they are important, but not urgent in the pursuit of goal completion and fighting off the chicken switch. Therefore, you can expect that many will not take the time or energy to think thoroughly through this process. And thus is born the willpower dilemma and the continued on-going livelihood of pulling the chicken switch. Don't be one of those people. Choose otherwise.

Step Seven – Accountability.

Maintain accountability

Accountability is twofold. Fold number one is a personal, private responsibility you have to hold yourself answerable to your commitments in pursuit of your desired outcomes. That will take willpower. No worries because you paid the price early to insure you had knowledge, desire, awareness, choice, commitment, and practice, so when accountability time shows up, you have a strong foundation to hold to when willpower weans and the chicken switch shows up.

Fold number two is the public announcement of your desired outcome. It's the liable side of things you put on yourself by enlisting others to help you push through and keep willpower high when temptation arises. By making your desired outcome known to others, you rig the anti-chicken switch system in your favor. Example: if others know you are not eating sugary foods, then whether in public or private, you are increasing the chances of staying away from sugar.

In addition, at an even more core level, the why of why this model works lies in the fact that the model teaches becoming committed to being a person of my word. You make and keep promises. That is who you are. That is who you want to be.

Kit Allowitz 2017

Special thanks to:

Kieran – I'd like to acknowledge my oldest son for pushing me to find and intrinsically create the willpower to finally write this book. I have been carrying around a file titled Don't Pull the Chicken Switch for over a decade. The material had seasoned and I was finally ready to write. He challenged me to write the material within a year. I did. Thank you son. Jack my wife – for the amazing support, love, patience, compassion, ideas, and willpower. To Kimball, Karigan and Creshel, thank you for dealing with my many chicken switches pulled, for listening to me go on and on about chicken switching conundrums and for always believing in me. To the many, many work colleagues over the years who inspired me, taught me, and shaped me. And finally for the life and accomplishments of Steve Prefontaine. I always wanted to run as fast as you!

Find tools, resources, workshop dates, coaching help, blog posts, articles, and willpower daily devotions at
www.chickenswitching.com

With questions, need help or to reach me:
kit.allowitz@chickenswitching.com

www.ingramcontent.com/pod-product-compliance
Lightning Source LLC
LaVergne TN
LVHW051606070426
835507LV00021B/2794